Abbas Schirmohammadi

WORKS Vol. 4

AF205919

Abbas Schirmohammadi

WORKS Vol. 4

Mein ultimatives Song Lyrics Archiv

Bibliografische Informationen der Deutschen Nationalbibliothek
Die Deutsche Nationalbibliothek verzeichnet diese Publikation in der
Deutschen Nationalbibliografie; detaillierte bibliografische Daten sind
im Internet über dnb.dnb.de abrufbar.

Printed in Germany

ISBN 978-3-7504-3607-7

Herstellung und Verlag: BoD – Books on Demand, Norderstedt

WORKS Vol. 4

Abbas Schirmohammadi

Inhaltsverzeichnis

6

Vorwort

Musik ist mein Leben. Das Klavier und die Gitarre sind meine besten Freunde. Bereits als 4-jähriger Knirps durfte ich am frühkindlichen Musikunterricht teilnehmen und entwickelte schnell eine große Leidenschaft für Takt, Rhythmus und Melodie. Anstatt sich ein neues Auto anzuschaffen, kauften mir meine Eltern damals auf Empfehlung meiner Klavierlehrerin ein nagelneues ED Seiler Klavier, das ich bis heute habe.

Als 7-Jähriger kam Schlagzeugunterricht auf einem eigenen Sabian & Remo Drumset dazu. Das Kinderzimmer war ab sofort ein Musikzimmer. Ich wurde von meinen Lehrern als „überaus begabt" bezeichnet und sehr gefördert. Schon mit 10 spielte ich einige komplizierte Werke der Klassik rauf und runter: Beethoven, Mozart, Schubert, Vivaldi und Verdi waren meine Favoriten.

Auch mein jüngerer Bruder hatte das Musik-Gen in sich, und so musizierten wir oft gemeinsam stundenlang. Mit 14 gefiel mir die Musik von Roxette, diese Songs wollte ich unbedingt spielen. Mein Klavierlehrer war davon zuerst nicht sonderlich begeistert, doch schließlich willigte er ein, dass wir uns auch mit modernerer Musik beschäftigten.

So lernte ich, ABBA, Beatles, Roxette, David Hasselhoff, EAV, OMD, Status Quo und sonstige Musik, die ich Anfang der 1990er kennenlernte und bis heute liebe, auf dem Klavier zu spielen. Parallel dazu ließ ich mich in Harmonielehre, Arrangement und Komposition ausbilden und hatte immer mehr Spaß am Musizieren. Ich lernte frei zu spielen. Jede Melodie, die ich hörte, produzierte ich problemlos nach. Synthesizer ermöglichten es uns, mit verschiedenen anderen Instrumenten außer Klavier und Schlagzeug zu musizieren.

Mit 17 komponierte ich meine ersten Stücke, ein Jahr später erschien mein Debüt-Album mit dem Titel „My Dreams of Harmony".

Mit 19 lernte ich E-Gitarre und Bass, beide Instrumente brachte ich mir selbst bei. Aktuell habe ich 8 E-Gitarren (Fender Telecaster) und einen Bass (Yamaha).

Mit der Zeit komponierte ich immer mehr. Waren es zuerst nur Instrumental-Songs, kamen dann immer mehr mit Texten (Lyrics) hinzu. Zuerst auf Deutsch, dann auf Englisch. Ich entwickelte eine Leidenschaft für Balladen und Pop Songs, aber mein Repertoire ist groß: Auch Rock, Blues, Jazz, Hip Hop, Swing, Heavy Metal, Funk, Schlager und andere Musikstile kann ich komponieren und spielen.

Zwischen 1998 und 2019 habe ich mehr als 1200 Songs komponiert, von denen viele bereits auf CDs erschienen sind, andere noch veröffentlicht werden. Diese Buchreihe „WORKS" beinhaltet mein musikalisches Lebenswerk, die Texte aller Songs, die ich in den letzten 20 Jahren geschrieben habe. Das Zusammentragen hat mir viel Freude bereitet und die Lyrics bedeuten mir sehr viel.

Die Bücher Vol. 1 bis Vol. 3 beinhalten meine Lyrics aus dem Zeitraum 1998 bis 2013. Alles alphabetisch sauber geordnet:
Vol. 1 = 1 - H
Vol. 2 = I - P
Vol. 3 = Q - Z

Vol. 4 bietet alle neuen Lyrics, die zwischen 2014 und 2019 entstanden sind.

Ich wünsche Ihnen viel Freude mit jenem Kompendium meiner musikalisch-lyrischen Arbeit!

Let´s Rock!
Abbas Schirmohammadi

1 - B

1000 MAL HAB ICH GELIEBT

EIN SONNENGRUSS AM MORGEN
DU IN MEINEM ARM
DER ERSTE TAG DES URLAUBS
DIE BALEAREN

EIN LEBEN VOLLER SONNE
SCHENK ICH NUR DIR
DEN SCHLÜSSEL MEINES HERZENS
UND AUCH DIE TÜR

1000 MAL HAB ICH GELIEBT
UND 1000 MAL GEHEULT
1000 MAL HAB ICH VERTRAUT
UND 1000 MAL BEREUT
NACH DEN 1000 MAL
WOLLT ICH NICHTS MEHR VON ALL DEM SCHEISS
LIEBE IST ZWAR SCHÖN
DOCH HAT SIE EINEN HOHEN PREIS

ICH HATTE MICH VERLOREN
KEINE LUST AUF MEHR
ICH LEBTE OHNE HOFFNUNG
ICH WAR SO LEER

DOCH DANN KAM ALLES BESSER
DENN DANN KAMST DU
DIE LIEBE MEINES LEBENS
JA, DAS BIST DU

1000 MAL HAB ICH GELIEBT
UND 1000 MAL GEHEULT
1000 MAL HAB ICH VERTRAUT
UND 1000 MAL BEREUT
NACH DEN 1000 MAL
WOLLT ICH NICHTS MEHR VON ALL DEM SCHEISS
LIEBE IST ZWAR SCHÖN
VERDAMMT HOCH ABER IST IHR PREIS

15 700 YEARS
(THE BLACK STONE OF DEATH)

15 700 YEARS
I´VE BEEN SEARCHING FOR THE BLACK STONE OF DEATH
16000 CANS OF BEERS
PLUGGED MY WAY AROUND THE WORLD ANYWHERE
THROUGH STICKS AND STONES
AND MAYBE BREAKING BONES

ALL THE POWER I COULD HAVE
IRRESISTIBLE I WOULD BE FOR ALL
SEARCHING, SLOWLY GETTING MAD
THE BLACK STONE OF DEATH IS SO FAR AWAY
BUT I JUST KNOW
SOME DAY IT WILL BE MINE

15 700 YEARS
AS TIME WILL TELL A TALE OF IMMORTALITY
16000 CANS OF BEER
TO FIGHT THE LIGHT AS ANGELS PASSING BY
13 MILLION DAYS AND MORE
I´M GONNA STAY FROM NOW
TO FIND THE STONE OF DEATH
ALL THE PANIC I IGNORE, KEEP GOING ON

I´M THE DEVIL IN DISGUISE
IF I´D SHOW MY FACE TO YOU EVERYWHERE
LOTS OF PEOPLE HAD TO DIE
SO I FLY A EAGLE UP IN THE AIR
THROUGH STICKY CLOUDS
AND FIRE IN THE SKY

15 700 YEARS
AS TIME WILL TELL A TALE OF IMMORTALITY
16000 CANS OF BEER
TO FIGHT THE LIGHT AS ANGELS PASSING BY
13 MILLION DAYS AND MORE
I´M GONNA STAY FROM NOW
TO FIND THE STONE OF DEATH
ALL THE PANIC I IGNORE, KEEP MOVING ON

17 YEARS

17 YEARS NOW HAVE GONE
17 YEARS NOW, SO LONG
GRANDMOTHER LEFT ME ALONE
ON MY OWN

SAD I WAS AND SO IN LOVE
GREETINGS TO GRANDMA ABOVE
PRAYING TO HER FOR MYSELF
I NEED HELP

17 YEARS NOW HAVE GONE
17 YEARS ON AND ON
LOOKING FOR YOU IN THE SHADES
IN MY DREAMS
NOWHERE YOU ARE, NOWHERE NEAR
SOMEWHERE YOU ARE BUT NOT HERE
AND SO I SEND ALL MY LOVE TO ABOVE

17 YEARS NOW HAVE GONE
FEELINGS ARE STILL VERY STRONG
DREADED THE DAY YOU FELL DOWN
ALL THE STAIRS

I WAS THE FIRST THERE TO HELP
I WAS TOO LATE AND I FELT
17 YEARS OF MY LIFE
NOW WERE GONE

THINKING OF YOU ALL THE TIME
DAYDREAMS AND VISIONS ARE MINE
WORLD IS ALRIGHT IN MY DREAMS
AS IT SEEMS
GRANDMA IS STILL IN MY HEART
YOU AND I WILL NEVER PART
LAUGHING WITH YOU ALL THE TIME
FEELING FINE

18 PRETTY LITTLE SEXY GIRLS

18 PRETTY LITTLE SEXY GIRLS
FROM 19 YEARS TO 21
THEY TRY TO BE A MODEL FOR THE WORLD
THEY GIVE IT UP BEFORE THEY´RE GONE
THEY FIGHT A CATFIGHT EVERY NIGHT
TO BE THE ONE, TO GET IT DONE
THEY DREAM A CINDERELLA DREAM
OF JOY AND FUN

MIDNIGHT IS ANOTHER NIGHT
IT NUMBER 2, THEN NUMBER 3
MOONLIGHT MAKES A PRETTY SIGHT
COURAGEOUS GIRLS ARE AFTER ME

18 PRETTY LITTLE SEXY GIRLS
FROM BLONDE TO BLACK, RED AND BRUNETTE
THEY COME TO ME AND SHOW ME ALL THEIR DREAMS
THEY SHOW ME ALL INSIDE THEIR JEANS
RESPECT I CANNOT HAVE FOR YOU
IF YOU JUST TRY TO MAKE ME FLY
AND ALL YOUR SEXUALITY
IS HAUNTING ME

MIDNIGHT IS ANOTHER NIGHT
IT NUMBER 8, THEN NUMBER 4
MOONLIGHT MAKES A PRETTY SIGHT
COURAGEOUS GIRLS KNOCK ON MY DOOR

JILL AND JENNY TRY TO MAKE ME SMILE
SENT ME PRIVATE PICTURES FOR MY EYES

18 PRETTY LITTLE SEXY GIRLS
I LOVE ´EM ALL, THEY ARE SO NICE
THE 18 PRETTY LITTLE SEXY GIRLS
WITH DIFFERENT NAMES, IT´S PARADISE
THEIR LEGS ARE HOT AND MAKE ME SWEAT
I´M DREAMING DREAMS INSIDE MY HEAD
A FANTASY NOW MUST COME TRUE
WITH ALL OF YOU

2, WE WERE 2

THE SKY IS SO BLUE
TAKE ME ALONG WITH YOU
NEW YORK, HERE WE COME
WASHINGTON, SO MUCH FUN

2, WE WERE 2
2, ME AND YOU
WE STROLLED ALONG, CARRIED ON

THOUSANDS OF DAYS
HUNDREDS OF WAYS
SEEING THE USA
TRAVELLING MORE
DAYS AT THE SHORE
NIGHTS AT THE BEACH, HURRAY
WHAT A SUNNY DAY!
2, WE WERE SO GAY

REMEMBER THE DAYS
TRAVELLING OUR WAYS
NEW YORK WAS SO GREAT
WASHINGTON WHERE WE STAYED

2, WE WERE 2
2, ME AND YOU
WE STROLLED ALONG, CARRIED ON

THOUSANDS OF DAYS
HUNDREDS OF WAYS
SEEING THE USA
TRAVELLING MORE
DAYS AT THE SHORE
NIGHTS AT THE BEACH, HURRAY
WHAT A SUNNY DAY!
2, WE WERE SO GAY

4 IT WAS SAID

5 NOT 4
I SLAM THE DOOR
GRAB MY COLT
I SHOOT THE BOLD
DEAL WENT WRONG
I´VE GOT TO GO
LEAVE THIS PLACE NOW FOR SURE

4 IT WAS SAID
NUMBER 5 DESTROYED ALL MY LIFE
I´M ON THE RUN
MANY DAYS FOR SURE NOW TO COME
4 IT WAS SAID
WELL PREPARED I WAS WITH MY FLIGHT
LEAVING THIS LAND TO HAWAII
ESCAPE WITH MY WIFE
5, 5 NOT 4, ONE TOO MUCH

DEAL WENT WRONG
I LOST MY WAY
ON THE RUN FOR A DAY

DAYS ARE BLACK
FROM BED TO BED
LOST MY LIFE
MY KIDS, MY WIFE
DEAL WENT WRONG
WAS 5 NOT 4
SEE ME RUN DOOR TO DOOR

4 IT WAS SAID
NUMBER 5 HE CHANGED ALL MY LIFE
I´M ON THE RUN
MANY DAYS FOR SURE NOW TO COME
4 IT WAS SAID
WELL PREPARED I WAS WITH MY FLIGHT
LEAVING THIS LAND TO HAWAII
ESCAPE WITH MY WIFE
5, 5 NOT 4, 1 TOO MUCH

5 LADIES IN ONE BED

5 PRETTY LADIES
LIVING IN ONE HOUSE
DRINKING SWEET RED WINE AND BAILEYS
WITH THEIR WELL FORMED LIPS AND MOUTHS
IN THIS RED HOT SEXY HOUSE

NO PETER PERFECT
NO DAVID B.'S AROUND
5 HORNY LADIES
AND THEY JUST PLAY IT OUT

TAKE YOUR TIME AND ENJOY
SOME GAMES YOU WON'T BELIEVE
BLONDE GOES RED, DARK GOES BROWN
I WATCH AND CANNOT LEAVE
PLAYING SOME GAMES
NEVER BELIEVED IN NAMES
MAKING ME SMILE
MAKING MY LIFE WORTHWHILE

NO PRETTY BOY TOYS
I CAN'T SEE JUST ONE
WELL, THE LADIES MAKE ME WONDER
WHY THEY LIVE AT 5 ALONE
WITHOUT BEARDS AND 5 OF DONGS

BUT THEY HAVE CHOICES
WHAT THEY JUST USE INSTEAD
5 PRETTY LADIES
ARE PLAYING IN ONE BED

TAKE YOUR TIME AND ENJOY
SOME GAMES YOU WON'T BELIEVE
BLONDE GOES RED, DARK GOES BROWN
I WATCH AND CANNOT LEAVE
PLAYING SOME GAMES
NEVER BELIEVED IN NAMES
MAKING ME SMILE
MAKING MY LIFE WORTHWHILE

A SUPERMAN LIKE YOU

I SEE YOU THERE
JUST LIKE A SUPERMAN IN THE AIR
SO MANY GUYS I HAVE TRIED
BUT THEY ARE FULL OF LIES

THEY'RE REALLY NOTHING FOR ME
THEY HAVE NO HEART OF GOLD
I DON'T HAVE PLANS TO LIVE WITH THEM
BECOMING OLD

WAS SEARCHING FOR A SUPERMAN LIKE YOU
A HEART OF GOLD WHOSE LOVE IS REALLY TRUE
I FOUND YOU ON THIS RAINY DAY
I DIDN'T CRY, I DIDN'T SAY GOODBYE
I COULDN'T TAKE ANOTHER DIRTY LIE
AND NOW WITH YOU I WANNA STAY

I SEE YOU THERE
YOU ARE MY SUPERMAN IN THE AIR
YOU'RE SHINING BRIGHT
LIKE A DIAMOND EARRING IN THE NIGHT

I DREAM OF LIVING WITH YOU
UNTIL THE END OF TIME
AND NOW IT'S ONLY UP TO YOU
TO MAKE ME SHINE

WAS SEARCHING FOR A SUPERMAN LIKE YOU
A HEART OF GOLD WHOSE LOVE IS REALLY TRUE
I FOUND YOU ON THIS RAINY DAY
I DIDN'T CRY, I DIDN'T SAY GOODBYE
I COULDN'T TAKE ANOTHER DIRTY LIE
AND NOW WITH YOU I WANNA STAY

A SUPERSTAR LIFE

PLAYING THE TRUMPET
DRINKING SOME WINE
WATCHING TV FEELING FINE

KISSING MY GIRLFRIENDS
PAYING THE BILLS
LIVING NEAR HOLLYWOOD HILLS

A HOUSE SOLID GOLD LIKE MY CAR
DIAMONDS FOR YOU, HERE THEY ARE
A SUPERSTAR LIFE CAN BE HARD
YOU HAVE TO LIVE AND LIVE IT SMART

SLEEPING 2 HOURS
SMOKING SOME WEED
LIVING A LIFE FULL OF SPEED

1 MAN, 10 LADIES
THAT´S WHO I AM
I TAKE THE GLASS OF CHAMPAGNE

A CINEMA SHOW JUST FOR ME
FLYING ALONE, I CAN SEE
AND FEEL WHAT IS LOVE EVERY DAY
RIGHT THERE ON TOP I´M HERE TO STAY
RIGHT THERE ON TOP I´M HERE TO STAY
RIGHT THERE ON TOP I´M HERE TO STAY

ADONIS ISN´T YOU

WELL, ADONIS ISN´T YOU
SKINNY SLIM AND LOOKING SO HAUNTED
I CAN SEE A BITTER POINT
THAT´S A WORTHLESS JOINT NO ONE WANTED
SWEET MARINDA LET YOU GO
SLAPPED YOUR DREAMS AND DOWN WENT THE SHOW
DOWN THE CORNER THERE´S A DOG
LIVING NOW WITH YOU ON THE ROAD

WELL, NOW ADONIS ISN´T YOU
BETTER UNDERSTAND IT IS TRUE
THE SHADY DEMONS IN THE DARK
BLOWING UP YOUR MIND AND YOUR HEART
ADONIS IS JUST IN YOUR HEAD
PRETTY LADIES NOT IN YOUR BED
THEY NEVER EVER COME TO YOU
THEY NEVER EVER GIVE YOUR LOVE TO YOU

WELL, ADONIS ISN´T YOU
NO, YOU DON´T, IT´S TRUE YOU´RE A LONER
WILL THERE EVER BE ONE GIRL?
LYING IN YOUR BED SHE WILL GO NOW
SWEET MARINDA, WHAT A SHAME!
LEFT YOU IN A JUNGLE OF RAIN
AS THE SUN IS GOING DOWN
MIRROW SHOWS THE LIFE OF A CLOWN

WELL, NOW ADONIS ISN´T YOU
BETTER UNDERSTAND IT IS TRUE
THE SHADY DEMONS IN THE DARK
BLOWING UP YOUR MIND AND YOUR HEART
ADONIS IS JUST IN YOUR HEAD
PRETTY LADIES NOT IN YOUR BED
THEY NEVER EVER COME TO YOU
THEY NEVER EVER GIVE YOUR LOVE TO YOU

AM STRAND VON NIRGENDWO
(ROMEO & JULIA)

AM STRAND VON NIRGENDWO
IN DER BOCCA-BAR
FERN VOM PARADIES
ICH TRINK AUF ROMEO UND AUF JULIA
ICH VERMISSE SIE, ICH VERMISSE SIE

DENK AN DIE SCHÖNE ZEIT MIT IHR ZURÜCK
SCHÜTTE HINAB DEN FRUST
UND TRÄUM VOM GLÜCK

IN DER BOCCA-BAR AM STRAND VON NIRGENDWO
STEHT EIN RICHTIG FESCHER ROMEO
MÖCHTEST DU HEUT ABEND TANZEN NUR MIT MIR?
ALLES WAS DU SIEHST GEHÖRT NUR DIR
DIESEN EINEN TANZ MIT ROMEO VERGISST DU NIE

ICH SEH DICH VOR MIR STEHEN
UND ICH SCHAU DICH AN
NAH AM PARADIES
OH MEINE JULIA, DU BIST WUNDERSCHÖN!
LONDON, ROM, PARIS - ICH ZEIG DIR DIE WELT

ALLES WAS DIR GEFÄLLT UND SO VIEL MEHR
ALLES FÜR EINEN KUSS
UND NOCH VIEL MEHR

IN DER BOCCA-BAR AM STRAND VON NIRGENDWO
DA STEH ICH, EIN FESCHER ROMEO
DEINE AUGEN SPIELEN TANGO NUR MIT MIR
JULIA, DIE WELT GEHÖRT NUR DIR
DIESE EINE NACHT MIT ROMEO VERGISST DU NIE

HEISS IST DIE NACHT
UND SCHNELL DER HIMMEL KLAR
ROMEO IST VERLIEBT IN JULIA

AND AS THE NIGHT IS GETTING DARKER NOW

SWEET LIES IN YOUR EYES
WELL, IT´S TIME TO SAY GOODBYE
I DON´T CARE ONE MORE TRY
IT IS OVER NOW FOR SURE

QUITE AS SEXY YOU ARE
AND MY FRIENDS THINK I´M THE ONE
YOU´RE JUST OUT FOR MY MONEY
AND YOUR FUN

AND AS THE NIGHT IS GETTING DARKER NOW
I WILL GO, YES, I GO
I WILL BE FREE AGAIN AND HAPPY NOW
FOR THE THINGS I DON´T KNOW
HERE I GO UP AND AWAY
KNOWING MY TIME WITH YOU IS OVER NOW
AND THIS ONE CRAZY SHOW
COMES TO AN END

I KNOW WHO YOU´VE BEEN
AND THE TRUTH IS HARD TO TAKE
WELL, THE WOMAN I´VE SEEN
WAS A BLOND EXPENSIVE FAKE

YOU BETRAYED ME NOT ONCE
WITH SOME GUYS YOU´VE BEEN AWAY
AND YOU´RE SPENDING MY MONEY
EVERY DAY

AND AS THE NIGHT IS GETTING DARKER NOW
I WILL GO, YES, I GO
I WILL BE FREE AGAIN AND HAPPY NOW
FOR THE THINGS I DON´T KNOW
HERE I GO UP AND AWAY
KNOWING MY TIME WITH YOU IS OVER NOW
AND THIS ONE CRAZY SHOW
COMES TO AN END

ANGEL

ANGEL, YOU´RE MY ANGEL
YOU´RE MY DARLING
YOU´RE MY LOVE
ANGEL, BLUE-EYED ANGEL
YOU´RE MY BABY
ALL MY LOVE

TAKE ME, PRETTY BABY
MAKE ME HAPPY
GIVE ME LOVE
KISS ME AND JUST HOLD ME
YOU´RE MY ANGEL
YOU´RE MY LOVE

ANGEL, WHEN I HOLD YOU
WHEN I KISS YOU
YOU ARE MINE
ANGEL, WHEN I´M LONELY
WHEN I MISS YOU
ALL THE TIME

TAKE ME, PRETTY BABY
MAKE ME HAPPY
GIVE ME LOVE
KISS ME AND JUST HOLD ME
YOU´RE MY ANGEL
YOU´RE MY LOVE

NOT FAR AWAY
WE WALK AWAY
FROM ALL THOSE LIES OF TODAY
HONESTLY CUTE
CHEMISTRY´S GOOD
SMILING FOR TWO
ME AND YOU

ANIMATION FANTASY

I LOOK INTO YOUR EYES
AND I CAN´T LET YOU GO
WANT YOU TO SHOW ME
YOU AIN´T GONNA KNOW
I´M MORE THAN JUST A MAN
ONLY YOU MAY IT FEEL
ANIMATION FANTASY IS REAL

I TAKE YOUR HAND
AND WE FLY, FLY AWAY
I KISS YOUR LIPS
AND WE FLY FOR A DAY
THE ANIMATION FANTASY
IS MORE THAN A DREAM
WE FLY AWAY INTO ANOTHER SCENE
AND SOON YOU KNOW REALITY´S A DREAM

AS ANIMATION MAN
I´M ALIVE PRETTY STRONG
I´M HAVING FUN
WITH MY GIRL NUMBER 1
THE ANIMATION MAN´S
FULL OF LOVE JUST FOR YOU
WANNA SEE THE SUNSHINE PRETTY BLUE?

I TAKE YOUR HAND
AND WE FLY, FLY AWAY
I KISS YOUR LIPS
AND WE FLY FOR A DAY
THE ANIMATION FANTASY
IS MORE THAN A DREAM
WE FLY AWAY INTO ANOTHER SCENE
AND SOON YOU KNOW REALITY´S A DREAM

AWAKE FOR MR. JAKE

MONDAY MORNING SUN
KISSING ME AWAKE
THE WEEKEND IS DONE
15 AFTER 8
STILL I´VE GOT SOME TIME
WITH YOU IN MY BED

PLAYING SOME GAMES NOW
YOU AND I
COWBOY AND BEAUTY
MAKE ME FLY
NEARLY 1 HOUR
I´M WITH YOU
NOW I´M AWAKE
FOR MR. JAKE

FRIDAY EVENING MOON
KISSING ME GOODNIGHT
AWAY IN MY ROOM
WEEKEND, HERE I COME
TIME TO ROLL THE DICE
AND TIME FOR SOME FUN

PLAYING GOOD GAMES NOW
YOU AND I
TEACHER AND STUDENT
MAKE ME FLY
TIL MONDAY MORNING
I´M WITH YOU
NOW I´M AWAKE
FOR MR. JAKE

AWAY THE SAND

AWAY THE SAND
AWAY THIS LAND
MY LOVE, I WON´T LEAVE YOU NOW

THE TIME WE HAD
THE GOOD AND BAD
AWAY IN THIS LAND
AWAY IN THE SAND OF GOLD

PLANE GOES UP AND AWAY
CRYING TEARS AGAIN
I WILL MISS YOU AGAIN
I´LL BE BACK FOR SURE
WE WILL MARRY AND MORE
LIVE A LIFE OF JOY
MAKE A GIRL AND A BOY
I´M IN LOVE WITH YOU

YOUR EYES LIKE MINE
ONE KISS, ONE WINE
ONE DAY I WON´T BE AWAY

AWAY THE SAND
WE LEAVE THIS LAND
OUR LOVE WILL BE STRONG
WE KEEP MOVING ON TO STAY

PLANE GOES UP AND AWAY
CRYING TEARS AGAIN
I WILL MISS YOU AGAIN
I´LL BE BACK FOR SURE
WE WILL MARRY AND MORE
LIVE A LIFE OF JOY
MAKE A GIRL AND A BOY
I´M IN LOVE WITH YOU

BABY, I CAN´T

TEARS IN MY EYES
YOU CAN´T DO THE THINGS OTHERS DO
GETTING A BOY I WANT FROM YOU

TELL ME WHAT´S WRONG
CAN YOU FEEL THE POISON IN YOU?
HEALTHY YOU LOOK BUT THAT´S NOT TRUE

HOW CAN IT BE?
I BELIEVED IN YOU
IT´S NOT MY FAULT
WHAT CAN I SAY?

BABY, I CAN´T, I CAN´T BELIEVE IN LOVE
BABY, I TRIED BUT YOU´RE NOT GOOD ENOUGH
BABY, I CAN´T, I CAN´T GO ON WITH YOU
I DON´T WANT THIS SHIT COME TRUE

HANDSOME AND STRONG
LIKE THE MAN WHO´S SINGING THIS SONG
FULL OF RESPECT FROM ALL THE BOYS

ONE FOR THE GIRLS
AS HE RIDES AND DIVES ROUND THE WORLD
BUT I BELIEVE I HAVE NO CHOICE

TO LEAVE BEHIND
WHAT I THOUGHT COULD BE
I LEAVE BEHIND
ONE PART OF ME

BABY, I CAN´T, I CAN´T BELIEVE IN LOVE
BABY, I TRIED BUT YOU´RE NOT GOOD ENOUGH
BABY, I CAN´T, I CAN´T GO ON WITH YOU
I DON´T WANT THIS SHIT COME TRUE

BABY, RUN AWAY!

I UNDERSTAND IT´S NOW MY FAULT
WE FUSS AND FIGHT UNTIL THE SLEEPING MODE
THE TIME HAS CHANGED AND SO HAVE I
YOU BETTER STOP IT NOW TO MAKE ME CRY

IMPOSSIBLE TO TALK OR TO REGRET
TO LOVE ANOTHER ONE
YOU BETTER RUN AWAY FROM ME NOW

BABY, RUN AWAY!
BETTER RUN AWAY, BABY, RUN AWAY!
LISTEN TO THE WORDS I SAY
BABY, RUN AWAY OUT INTO THE DARK OF THE NIGHT!
DON´T YOU DARE TO COME AGAIN
BETTER RUN AWAY
BABY, RUN AWAY! BE A RUNAWAY
HEAR MY WORDS AND READ MY LIPS
BETTER RUN AWAY
BABY, RUN AWAY INTO THE NIGHT!

I UNDERSTAND YOU BROKE MY BONES
YOU LIED TO ME JUST LIKE A ROLLING STONE
I CAN´T DENY MY TIME WITH YOU
WAS SOMETHING SPECIAL AS MY LOVE FOR YOU

WAS STRONGER THAN YOUR LIES
I DIDN´T CARE, I DIDN´T HEAR THEM ALL
BUT SOMETHING DEEP INSIDE CLOSED THE DOOR

BABY, RUN AWAY!
BETTER RUN AWAY, BABY, RUN AWAY!
LISTEN TO THE WORDS I SAY
BABY, RUN AWAY OUT INTO THE DARK OF THE NIGHT!
DON´T YOU DARE TO COME AGAIN
BETTER RUN AWAY
BABY, RUN AWAY! BE A RUNAWAY
HEAR MY WORDS AND READ MY LIPS
BETTER RUN AWAY
BABY, RUN AWAY INTO THE NIGHT!

BACK IN LIFE AGAIN

I COME AROUND
YOU STRIP AND PLAY
AND MAKE MY WORLD
SO GOOD AGAIN

NOBODY KNOWS
I´M HERE WITH YOU
A SECRET LIFE
A RENDEZVOUS

WHEN I´M ALONE
AS MY WIFE´S GROWING OLD, NUMB AND GREY
I NEED MY LIFE
GETTING BETTER AGAIN SO TO SAY
AND IN THIS WORLD
WHERE MY DREAMS CAN COME TRUE I´M A MAN
SO YOUNG AND STRONG AGAIN
I AM BACK IN LIFE AGAIN

WHAT´S YOUNG THAT´S GOOD
I´M SORRY, WIFE
I NEED THIS DRIVE
TO STAY ALIVE

YOU´LL NEVER KNOW
AND I DON´T CARE
I LOVE YOU STILL
WHEN YOU´RE NOT THERE

WHEN I´M ALONE
AS MY WIFE´S GROWING OLD, NUMB AND GREY
I NEED MY LIFE
GETTING BETTER AGAIN SO TO SAY
AND IN THIS WORLD
WHERE MY DREAMS CAN COME TRUE I´M A MAN
SO YOUNG AND STRONG AGAIN
I AM BACK IN LIFE AGAIN

BALLER-BALLER-BALLERMANN

STIMMUNG, STIMMUNG, BALLERMANN
DIE PARTYNACHT DIE FÄNGT JETZT AN
RINGELREIHEN UND BLINDE KUH, DIE AUGEN ZU
HÜBSCHE HÄNDE ÜBERALL
DIE MENGE TOBT IM DONNERHALL
LIRUM LARUM LÖFFELSTIEL, HEUT NACHT GEHT VIEL

BALLER-BALLER-BALLERMANN, BALLERMANN, BALLERMANN
BALLER-BALLER-BALLERMANN
ICH ZIEH DIE RICHTIGE HOSE AN
BALLER-BALLER-BALLERMANN, BALLERMANN, BALLERMANN
BALLER-BALLER-BALLERMANN
ICH ZIEH DAS RICHTIGE T-SHIRT AN

WÄHREND ICH HIER OBEN STEH
UND ALL DIE HÜBSCHEN BUNNYS SEH
HIER AM PARTY-BALLERMANN, DAS TÖRNT MICH AN
ALL DIE NACKTEN ZENTIMETER
WIRKEN AUF DES MANNES´ PETER
JEDE NACHT AUFS NEUE STEHT ER WIE ´NE EINS

BALLER-BALLER-BALLERMANN, BALLERMANN, BALLERMANN
BALLER-BALLER-BALLERMANN
ICH ZIEH DIE RICHTIGE JACKE AN
BALLER-BALLER-BALLERMANN, BALLERMANN, BALLERMANN
BALLER-BALLER-BALLERMANN
ICH ZIEH DIE RICHTIGE MÜTZE AN

KOMM ICH DANN UM 6 INS BETT
DANN SCHLAF ICH ERST MAL SUPERFETT
NACH DEM SEX KOMM ICH ZUR RUH, UND WER BIST DU?
NÄCHSTE NACHT AM BALLERMANN
UND WENN ICH DICH NICHT FINDE DANN
SCHAU ICH IN DIE MENGE, UND DANN AB DAFÜR!

BALLER-BALLER-BALLERMANN, BALLERMANN, BALLERMANN
BALLER-BALLER-BALLERMANN
ICH HEIZ EUCH EIN AM BALLERMANN
BALLER-BALLER-BALLERMANN, BALLERMANN, BALLERMANN
BALLER-BALLER-BALLERMANN
ICH BIN DER KING VOM BALLERMANN

BERGGIPFEL UND TALFAHRT UND ZURÜCK

HEUTE IST EIN TAG WIE GESTERN
NUR DIE SONNE SCHEINT
DU HAST MIR VERZIEHEN
MEIN DARLING, JA, ES TUT MIR LEID
LASS UNS WIEDER LIEB UND GUT SEIN
KOMM IN MEINEN STARKEN ARM
UNSERE LIEBE FÜREINANDER
HÄLT UNS WARM

ALL DIE JAHRE
ALL DIE SORGEN, ALL DAS GLÜCK
BERGGIPFEL UND TALFAHRT UND ZURÜCK
IMMER INTENSIV
DAS LIEBESKARUSSELL
DREHT SICH MANCHMAL LANGSAM
MANCHMAL SCHNELL
DOCH MEIN KLEINES HERZ
LIEBT NUR DICH GANZ ALLEIN

WENN SICH UNSERE LIPPEN KÜSSEN
BLEIBT MEIN HERZ FAST STEHEN
WENN SICH UNSERE KÖRPER TREFFEN
MÖCHT ICH NICHT MEHR GEHEN
FREUDENTRÄNEN VOLLER LIEBE
SCHENK ICH DIR, MEIN SONNENSCHEIN
NUR MIT DIR ZUSAMMEN
KANN ICH GLÜCKLICH SEIN

ALL DIE JAHRE
ALL DIE SORGEN, ALL DAS GLÜCK
BERGGIPFEL UND TALFAHRT UND ZURÜCK
IMMER INTENSIV
DAS LIEBESKARUSSELL
DREHT SICH MANCHMAL LANGSAM
MANCHMAL SCHNELL
DOCH MEIN KLEINES HERZ
LIEBT NUR DICH GANZ ALLEIN

BIG ADVENTURES IN THE SKY

UP IN THE MORNING SKY
IN THE DIZZY LIGHT
BIRDIES ARE FLYING OVER YOU
THEY DIDN'T SLEEP TONIGHT
AND THEY FEEL ALRIGHT
WONDERING WHERE THEY ARE GOING TO

IF WE FOLLOW OUR DREAM
DREAMS ARE REALLY TO BE SEEN
NOT BIRDS AT ALL

BIG ADVENTURES IN THE SKY
THEY FLY AWAY INTO THEIR GLORY
STRONG CONFESSIONS FLYIN' HIGH
IT'S NO MORE PLACE ROUND HERE TO WORRY
AND THEN AWAY

UP IN THE MORNING BLUE
AND ALL OVER YOU
WATCHING THE JOURNEY OF THE DAY
WELL, IS IT REALLY TRUE?
THE GOING-OVER-CREW
SEARCHING A BETTER PLACE TO STAY

IF WE FOLLOW OUR BRO
HE JUST SHOWS US WHERE TO GO
TO SMILE AGAIN

BIG ADVENTURES IN THE SKY
THEY FLY AWAY INTO THEIR GLORY
STRONG CONFESSIONS FLYIN' HIGH
IT'S NO MORE PLACE ROUND HERE TO WORRY
AND THEN AWAY

BIGGER LOVE

A LONELY NIGHT
A LONELY NIGHT HERE WITH YOU
A PRETTY DATE
BUT THIS IS SO SAD AND TRUE

2 DIFFERENT PEOPLE
JUST TRY TO FIND WHAT IS LOVE
THERE AIN´T NO WAY
TO THE STARS ABOVE

A LONELY NIGHT IT WAS FOR ME AGAIN AND FOR YOU
ONE MORE TIME WE TRIED OUR BEST
TO MAKE OUR BODIES FLY INTO THE BLUE
BIGGER LOVE I TRY TO FIND
I´M COMING CLOSER NOW TO MY DREAM
SWEETER LOVE, I KNOW YOU´RE SOMEWHERE THERE
AND WAIT FOR ME, I´M AFTER YOU

YOUR EMPTY FACE
YOUR EMPTY FACE MAKES ME SAD
A PRETTY GIRL YOU ARE
BUT NOT IN MY BED

A WORLD OF DATING APPS
SO UNREAL, SO UNREAL
I TRY TO FEEL
BUT NO LOVE I FEEL

BIGGER LOVE
A LONELY NIGHT IT WAS FOR ME AGAIN AND FOR YOU
YOU AND I, WE TRIED OUR BEST
TO MAKE OUR BODIES FLY INTO THE BLUE
BIGGER LOVE I TRY TO FIND
I´M COMING CLOSER NOW TO MY DREAM
SWEETER LOVE, I KNOW YOU´RE SOMEWHERE THERE
AND WAIT FOR ME, I´M AFTER YOU

BITTE VERGIB MIR

ICH SITZ DAHEIM
ALS ES KLINGELT AN DER TÜR
DU SCHAUST MICH AN
UND ICH SCHÄME MICH DAFÜR
VATER, VERGIB MIR WAS ICH TAT
SIEH MEINE TRÄNEN UND ICH SAG:

BITTE VERGIB MIR, LASS MICH FREI
ES TUT MIR LEID, ICH WAR SO KLEIN
DRÜCK MICH GANZ FEST
JA, ICH LIEF FORT VOR LANGER ZEIT
WOLLTE NUR WEG VON ALL DEM STREIT
DRÜCK MICH GANZ FEST, BITTE VERZEIH
ES TUT SO WEH, ICH FÜHL MICH FREI

ICH WAR EIN KIND
WUSSTE NIE WAS HOFFNUNG WAR
IHR FÜHRTET KRIEG
NACH DER SCHEIDUNG WAR MIR KLAR
UNSERE FAMILIE BRACH ENTZWEI
ICH WOLLTE FRIEDEN GANZ ALLEIN

BITTE VERGIB MIR, SIEH MICH AN
AUS MIR GEWORDEN IST EIN MANN
GANZ SO WIE DU
HAB EINE FRAU UND EINEN SOHN
KOMM ENDLICH REIN, SIE WARTEN SCHON
ICH BIN SO FREI, KOMM HER, MEIN SOHN
DAS IST DEIN OPA, SAG HALLO

BLONDE ONE IS THE BEST

CHICKS ARE ON THE DANCEFLOOR
SOME PRETTY ONES ALL AROUND
AND HERE IS MR. AWESOME
A-RAPPIN' ON TO THE SOUND
NOT INTERESTED IN BARFIGHTS
NOT INTERESTED TO DANCE
I'M A HANDSOME FIGARO
MASTER OF LOVE AND ROMANCE
IF YOU ARE INTERESTED
JUST LOOK IN MY MAGIC EYES
I'M GONNA MAKE YOU
HAPPY AND DATE YOU
SHOW YOU A HORNY SENSATION
A MAGIC SURPRISE

BLONDE ONE'S REALLY CRAZY
SHE'S FOLLOWING WITH 2
ANOTHER PRETTY LADIES
WE'RE LEAVING INTO THE BLUE
GINA, JENNY AND SUNSHINE
ALL ARE SEXY AND YOUNG
SHOWING THEM MY LIMOUSINE
GETTING ME READY TO COME
IN THIS CAR OF MAGIC
THE PARTY GETS WILD AND WET
DRIVER IS DRIVING
LIMOUSINE'S RIDING
AS I HAVE FUN
AS THE CHICKS GET AROUSED IN MY BED

CAR IS DRIVING FAST
I'M RIGHT AT ON MY BEST
AND I HAVE TO SAY:
WELL, THE BLONDE ONE IS THE BEST
AWESOME IS MY TIME
HANDS AND LIPS ARE ALL MINE
BLONDE DID PERFECT WORK
NOW I'M FEELING SUPER FINE

NEXT NIGHT ON THE DANCEFLOOR
SOME PRETTY GIRLS STILL AROUND
AGAIN IT´S MR. AWESOME
A-RAPPIN´ ON TO THE SOUND
NOT INTERESTED IN FRIENDSHIPS
NOT INTERESTED IN DARTS
I´M A HANDSOME FIGARO
OWNER OF ACES IN CARDS
IF YOU ARE TOO HORNY
AND CANNOT JUST WAIT NO MORE
LEAVING THIS PLACE
AND FLYING TO SPACE
A GENTLEMAN SHOWS YOU THE WAY
TO MY LIMOUSINE´S DOOR

BLONDE ONE´S REALLY CRAZY
SHE´S FOLLOWING ME WITH 4
ANOTHER SEXY LADIES
AND THEY ARE ALL OUT FOR MORE
GINA, LISA AND MARY
SWEET OKSANA, MARIE
I´M THE GOLDEN SUPERMAN
LIVING SO HAPPY AND FREE
GIRLS ARE GETTING NAKED
SOME BODIES OF LOVE I FEEL
HEAVENLY GATES
AND SILVERING SHADES
I´M CALLING, I´M FALLING
THE LOVE AND THE JOY IS SO REAL

CAR IS DRIVING FAST
I´M RIGHT AT ON MY BEST
AND I HAVE TO SAY:
WELL, THE BLONDE ONE IS THE BEST
AWESOME IS MY TIME
HANDS AND LIPS ARE ALL MINE
BLONDE DID PERFECT WORK
NOW I´M FEELING SUPER FINE

BLUE MOON

WAITING, SOMEONE´S WAITING
ENDLESS HOURS, MANY DAYS
TURNING AS COOL WATER
DROPPING DOWN ON HIS RAINY HEAD

BREAKING, DAWN IS BREAKING
AS HE´S WAITING FOR MY HAND
ONLY ONE NIGHT ONLY
COMES THE SUNSHINE TO BE HIS FRIEND

RED, PURPLE, YELLOW, GREEN AND WHITE
RAINBOW UP IN THE NIGHT
BLUE MOON AND 20 SHOOTING LIGHTS
MAKING THEIR WAY TONIGHT
LEFT, RIGHT AND UP, DOWN, IN BETWEEN
BLUE MOON AIN´T JUST A DREAM
COOL-HOT THE SPOTS ARE IN THE NIGHT
BLUE MOON IS HERE TONIGHT

SMILING, NOW HE´S SMILING
CAUSE THE RAINBOW STAYS TONIGHT
TURNING, NO MORE BURNING
DAWN IS BREAKING, HERE COMES THE LIGHT

RED, PURPLE, YELLOW, GREEN AND WHITE
RAINBOW UP IN THE NIGHT
BLUE MOON AND 20 SHOOTING LIGHTS
MAKING THEIR WAY TONIGHT
LEFT, RIGHT AND UP, DOWN, IN BETWEEN
BLUE MOON AIN´T JUST A DREAM
COOL-HOT THE SPOTS ARE IN THE NIGHT
BLUE MOON IS HERE TONIGHT

BREAKING BONES

I WORK FROM 6 TO TEA FOR TWO
COME HOME AND START ANOTHER DAY
AS THE SUN IS WAKING UP MY HEART
I PLAY SOME GAMES I WANNA PLAY
DESTROY A BUNCH OF SUPERSTARS
TIL IT´S TIME TO RISE AND START AGAIN
I´M 24 IN YEARS OF AGE
SOME PEOPLE CALL MY LIFE A STUPID GOLDEN CAGE
I MAY BE HONEST WHEN I SAY
I WALK MY GOLDEN LOVELY WAY
BETTER OFF I AM TO LIVE MY DAY

BREAKING DIFFERENT BONES
A PILE OF COCE UP IN MY NOSE
SEXY ARE THE GIRLS, I TAKE A BREAK
A SHOOTER GAME IS STRATEGY
I´M ON MY WAY TO HISTORY
DON´T YOU EVER DARE TO CALL ME FAKE
SHAME ON YOU, MY RIGHT IS HARD TO TAKE
GET UP AND SMILE

A GAME OF CLANS AND DREAMS AND HOPE
A NIGHT OF SUNSHINE IN THE DARK
YES, I´M ON MY WAY TO LOSE MY HEART
AND THOUGH I´M DIFFERENT CAN YOU SEE
I´M REALLY HAPPY AS CAN BE
LIVE MY WAY MY LIFE NOT FOR THE STARS
MY FATHER CALLED ME YESTERDAY
TO SAY I´M REALLY NOT OK TO BE HIS SON
I SMASHED MY PHONE UP ON THE FLOOR
SO HE CAN´T CALL ME ANYMORE
SORRY DAD, RELATIONSHIP IS DONE

BREAKING DIFFERENT BONES
A PILE OF COCE UP IN MY NOSE
SEXY ARE THE GIRLS, I TAKE A BREAK
A SHOOTER GAME IS STRATEGY
I´M ON MY WAY TO HISTORY
DON´T YOU EVER DARE TO CALL ME FAKE
SHAME ON YOU, MY RIGHT IS HARD TO TAKE
GET UP AND SMILE

BUTTERFLIES OF TOKYO

THE BUTTERFLIES OF TOKYO
YELLOW, RED AND BLUE
THEY´RE FLYING FAST ALONG WITH ME
THIN THEY ARE AND CUTE
THE BUTTERFLIES OF TOKYO
SWIRRING ROUND MY HEAD
BELIEVE ME NOW OR NOT, IT SEEMS
WELL, I PREFER THE RED

RED BUTTERFLIES OF TOKYO
FOLLOWING ME CLOSE
NO MATTER WHAT DAYTIME IT IS
NO MATTER WHERE IT SHOWS
THE BUTTERFLIES OF TOKYO
THEY ARE ALWAYS THERE
I´M SLEEPING IN A CORNER FIELD
THEY ARE EVERYWHERE

BUTTERFLIES, BUTTERFLIES OF TOKYO
THEY SEE, THEY RUN THE SHOW
ALL OVER TOKYO, NO MATTER WHERE I GO
I SEE THE BUTTERFLIES OF TOKYO
THE BUTTERFLIES OF TOKYO

THE BUTTERFLIES OF TOKYO
FLYING IN MY HEART
THE RED ONES AND SOME GREEN I LIKE
MORNING COMES TO START
I TAKE A WALK THROUGH TOKYO
TOKYO I LIKE
BESIDE ME, AROUND, EVERYWHERE
BUTTERFLIES I LIKE

BUTTERFLIES, BUTTERFLIES OF TOKYO
THEY SEE, THEY RUN THE SHOW
ALL OVER TOKYO, NO MATTER WHERE I GO
I SEE THE BUTTERFLIES OF TOKYO
THE BUTTERFLIES OF TOKYO

C - E

CAN´T FORGET

THERE´S SO MUCH I´VE BEEN GONE THROUGH
WHIRLING ROUND IN MY HEAD
ALL THE SWEET TIMES AND MEMORIES
WHILE I´M LYING IN BED

I´VE THROWN AWAY
HUNDREDS OF DAYS
I´VE LOST MY LIFE
IN THE SHADES

DRINKING SO MUCH CAUSE I CAN´T FORGET THE TIME
I CAN´T FORGET ALL THE GIRLS I THOUGHT WERE MINE
DARK SHADES OF BLACK HAUNTING ME BACK
CAN´T FORGET, CAN´T DENY ALL MY LIFE

ANY CHANCE OF A NEW START
ANY HOPE OF A TIME
I COULD MAKE IT MUCH BETTER
I COULD FEELIN´ SO FINE

SO MANY THOUGHTS
BRINGING ME DOWN
REALITY
SPINS ME ROUND

DRINKING SO MUCH CAUSE I CAN´T FORGET THE TIME
I CAN´T FORGET ALL THE GIRLS I THOUGHT WERE MINE
DARK SHADES OF BLACK HAUNTING ME BACK
CAN´T FORGET, CAN´T DENY ALL MY LIFE

GRANDMA, YOU WERE RIGHT
ALL YOUR WORDS WERE RIGHT
I WAS BLIND TO SEE YOU WERE RIGHT

CAR IN MY FACE, ALRIGHT

MANY BELIEVE IN LOVE
DON´T YOU JUST FEEL ENOUGH?
SEARCHING A GIRL FOR YOU
MAYBE THIS BLONDE CAN DO

TAKE ME AWAY
LEAVING TODAY
OUT OF MY MIND
LEAVING BEHIND

FANTASY, YOU AND ME
TAKE ME TO A LAND
HONESTY, CHANCE TO BE
LOOKING FOR A DANCE

RAINBOW IS WHITE AND BLACK
CLOUDS ARE IN BLUE AND RED
NOWHERE IS NEAR TONIGHT
CAR IN MY FACE, ALRIGHT

LONG LONELY ROADS
COLD EMPTY STROKES
OUT OF MY MIND
LEAVING BEHIND

FANTASY, YOU AND ME
TAKE ME TO A ROOM
HONESTY, CHANCE TO BE
I WILL BE THERE SOON

CASANOVA

I´M A CASANOVA, BABY
I´M WATCHING AFTER YOU
LOOKING FOR A PRETTY LADY
WELL, MAYBE IT IS YOU
I´M A CASANOVA LOVER
JUST READ IT IN THE BOOK
TAKE YOU AS MY NEWEST NUMBER
YOU´VE GOT THE WESTSIDE LOOK

DON´T ASK ME NO QUESTIONS, BABY
YOU´RE FREE TO BE THE ONE
BY MY SIDE FOREVER MAYBE
OR JUST AN HOUR LONG
I´M A CASANOVA HUNTER
MY LIFE IS FULL OF JOY
MAKE ME HAPPY, BE MY CENTRE
AND CASANOVA´S TOY

I´M NOW FOR SURE CASANOVA
COME NOW WITH ME FOR TONIGHT
SHOW WHAT YOU CAN, TAKE ME OVER
THIS´ WHAT I CALL PERFECT NIGHT

I´M A CASANOVA, BABY
I´M WATCHING AFTER YOU
LOOKING FOR A PRETTY LADY
WELL, MAYBE IT IS YOU
I´M A CASANOVA LOVER
JUST READ IT IN THE BOOK
TAKE YOU AS MY NEWEST NUMBER
YOU´VE GOT THE EASTSIDE LOOK

I´M NOW FOR SURE CASANOVA
COME NOW WITH ME FOR TONIGHT
SHOW WHAT YOU CAN, TAKE ME OVER
THIS´ WHAT I CALL PERFECT NIGHT

CATCH ANOTHER LIGHT

MY LIFE WILL END ANOTHER DAY
I DON´T KNOW HOW I LEAVE THIS WORLD AND FLY AWAY
I KNOW THE PATH I´M WALKING ON
IS BREAKING DOWN JUST LIKE A FLYING ROLLING STONE

I COULD LIVE ANOTHER DAY
BUT I´M HAPPY ON MY WAY

IN MY DREAMS I´M MOVING ON
INTO ANOTHER WAY OF LIFE
ENDING THIS FOR SURE TO FLY
I´M COMING, PARADISE
NO MORE CRYING IN THE NIGHT
AND NO MORE DUNGEONS IN MY MIND
I´M MOVING FORWARD NOW
TO CATCH ANOTHER LIGHT

MY LIFE WILL GO, DON´T WANNA STAY
CAUSE PLANET EARTH WAS JUST ANOTHER GIVE-AWAY
I DID MY BEST WITH ALL MY BALLS
BUT AS I TRIED I MISSED TO HEAR MY CURTAIN CALL

I AM OVER NOW FOR SURE
STOP THIS CRYING ON THE FLOOR

IN MY DREAMS I´M MOVING ON
INTO ANOTHER WAY OF LIFE
ENDING THIS FOR SURE TO FLY
I´M COMING, PARADISE
NO MORE CRYING IN THE NIGHT
AND NO MORE DUNGEONS IN MY MIND
I´M MOVING FORWARD NOW
TO CATCH ANOTHER LIGHT

AS MY FINAL DAY HAS COME
I WATCH UP INTO THE SUN
TAKE MY FINAL BREATH ON EARTH
AND FLY AWAY, I FLY AWAY

CHEATIN´ MARRIED MAN

YOUR HATE IS ENDLESS AS I TURN AROUND
CAUSE I SAID NO TO YOU
I´M LEAVING YOU
GOODBYE MY HANDBUILT HOUSE
IT´S SUCH A SHAME

I KNOW THAT THOMAS SPENT THE NIGHT WITH YOU
UNTIL THE MORNING LIGHT
AND WHAT YOU DID
YOU REALLY SHOULDN´T DO
THIS DREADED NIGHT

I PACK MY BAGS AND LEAVE THIS PLACE OF EMPTINESS
THAT´S IN YOUR HEART
THIS MARRIED MAN IS REALLY VERY SMART
DESTROYING TWO RELATIONSHIPS IN JUST ONE NIGHT
I KNOW HIS BRIDE

THIS MARRIED MAN IS SUCH A STUPID BLOKE
CAUSE I´M A LAWYER´S FRIEND
I MAKE HIM PAY THE BILLS
AND CRASH HIS HOPES
UNTIL HE´S DOWN

SWEET JENNY IS ANOTHER SEXY GIRL
BUT TOM, YOU DIDN´T KNOW
I HAD A LOT OF
NAUGHTY KIND OF FUN
FOR SWEET REVENGE

OH JENNY, JENNY, LET US PLAY THE LOVING GAME
PLEASE UNDERSTAND
YOUR THOMAS IS A CHEATIN´ MARRIED MAN
OH THOMAS, THOMAS, NOW YOU´VE SEEN THE END OF DAYS
I´M WATCHING YOU

HEY, IT´S OVER NOW
YOU BROKE MY HEART
AND MADE ME GO
LIES UP FROM THE START
I DIDN´T CARE
I DIDN´T KNOW

COMES THE NIGHT
(FIREMAN)

THE WORLD IS IN A MESS
PRETTY LADIES ALL AROUND
INSTEAD OF DRINKING BEER
THEY JUST PLAY AROUND
I´M SO HAPPY WHEN I SEE
ALL THE BODIES YOUNG AND SWEET
I CAN TOUCH THEM NOW
CAN YOU FEEL THE CURVES
AND CAN YOU FEEL THE HEAT AROUND THIS PLACE?
AN IRRESTIBLE FORCE
THAT´S CRASHING SOLID WALLS
AND OPENING SOME DOORS
I´M LIKE A FIREMAN
I LIKE THE FIRE, MAN
THE WORLD IS IN A MESS
I´M WAITING FOR A HURRICANE

COMES THE NIGHT AND I TALK TO YOU
WHERE AM I REALLY GOING TO?
SMILING CUTE AS YOU TALK TO ME
SHOW ME THINGS I JUST WANNA SEE

I´VE BEEN FROM BLONDE TO BLACK
PRETTY RED AND SWEET BRUNETTE
I NEARLY LOVE ´EM ALL
BUT I DON´T LIKE FAT
I WAS 13 AND 2 DAYS
WHEN I STARTED PLAYIN´ GAMES
WITH A GIRL NAMED JEN
SHE WAS MORE THAN JUST ANOTHER PRETTY FRIEND
SHE WAS SO HOT, SHE WAS 17, HA!
I LOVED HER ALL THE WAY
AND GAVE HER ALL MY LOVE
BECAME HER FIREMAN
I LOVED HER FIRE, MAN
WOULD SPEND A LOT OF MONEY
JUST TO SEE HER COME AGAIN

CALLING ALL THE LOVERS
JUST TO MEET ME IN THE NIGHT
CALLING, CALLING, CALLING
BETTER MAKE ME FEEL ALRIGHT
ALL THE PRETTY LADIES
AND-A-ALL THE HANDSOME MEN
HAVING FUN AND MAKING LOVE
UNTIL IT'S DAY AGAIN
CALLING ALL THE LOVERS
JUST TO MEET ME IN THE NIGHT
CALLING, CALLING, CALLING
BETTER MAKE ME FEEL ALRIGHT
ALL THE PRETTY LADIES
AND-A-ALL THE HANDSOME MEN
HAVING FUN AND MAKING LOVE
UNTIL IT'S DAY AGAIN

THE CHICKS ALL ON THE FLOOR
PRETTY LADIES IN A MESS
I HAD A NIGHT OF 4
UP TO 6 MY BEST
COMES THE DAY AND COMES THE WORK
7 HOURS ONCE AGAIN
EARN SOME BUCKS FOR ME
AND MY WIFE AND THE 2 CHILDREN
I'M A SO HARD WORKING MAN
I'M A PLAYBOY IN A SUIT
A SPECIAL KIND OF MAGIC MAKES ME LIVE MY MOOD
BECAME A FIRMAN
HOT GIRLS ON FIRE, MAN
THE NIGHT HAS COME
AND I JUST TURN INTO A HURRICANE

COMES THE NIGHT AND I TALK TO YOU
WHERE AM I REALLY GOING TO?
SMILING CUTE AS YOU TALK TO ME
SHOW ME THINGS I JUST WANNA SEE

CRAZY THOUGHTS IN YOUR MIND

SOME CRAZY THOUGHTS IN YOUR MIND
YOU ARE HELPLESS, FEELING BLIND
IT´S WHIRLING ROUND IN YOUR HEAD
SPOOKY DAYDREAMS MAKE ME SAD

VOICES NOW
FLYING ROUND IN YOUR HEAD ALONE
GOING DOWN
LIKE A TUMBLING ROLLING STONE

GUESS YOU´RE CRAZY NOW
GOING NOWHERE NOW
ARE YOU CLEAR TO SEE?
HELPING YOU IS ME
SOME CRAZY THOUGHTS IN YOUR MIND
CHANGE YOU ROUND AGAIN

SOME CRAZY THOUGHTS IN YOUR EYES
MAKE ME SHIVER, REALISE
THAT OUR ROAD IS NOW YOURS
I AM LEAVING OUR TOURS

CAN´T BELIEVE
WHAT HAS HAPPENED TO YOU, MY LOVE
SCARY GHOSTS
ARE MUCH STRONGER THAN ALL ABOVE

SEEMS YOU´RE CRAZY NOW
GOING NOWHERE NOW
ARE YOU CLEAR TO SEE?
HELPING YOU IS ME
SOME CRAZY THOUGHTS IN YOUR MIND
CHANGE YOU ROUND AGAIN

D´ARTAGNAN

D´ARTAGNAN - YOU´RE THE MAN OF THE STREET
TAKING CARE OF THE GUYS WANNA CHEAT
D´ARTAGNAN - YOU´RE THE MAN OF THE NIGHT
HERO OF THE POOR, FOR THE RIGHT

D´ARTAGNAN - YOU´RE THE REAL SUPERMAN
TAKING CARE OF THIS LAND AVALAN
D´ARTAGNAN - MR. X COMES YOUR WAY
SECONDS LATER, HEY, HE´S AWAY

FASTER AS A COLT
AND WORKING NOT FOR GOLD
FIGHTING EVERY NIGHT
´GAINST THE WRONG AND FOR THE RIGHT
BETTER THAN BIG THOR
AND SMASHING 1 TO 4
BAD GUYS DOIN´ WRONG IN THE NIGHT

D´ARTAGNAN - YOU´RE THE MAN, YOU´RE THE ONE
HITTING HARD AND THE STRANGERS ARE GONE
D´ARTAGNAN - KILLER FRED´S AFTER YOU
HAUNTING FOR YOUR LIFE, SHOULDN´T DO

D´ARTAGNAN - KILLER FRED´S NOW AWAY
WHERE HE´S NOW YOU DO KNOW, I DON´T SAY
YOU´RE MY MAN OF THE STREET - D´ARTAGNAN
YOU´RE THE BEST I´VE SEEN, SEE AND SAW

FASTER AS A COLT
AND WORKING NOT FOR GOLD
FIGHTING EVERY NIGHT
´GAINST THE WRONG AND FOR THE RIGHT
BETTER THAN BIG THOR
AND SMASHING 1 TO 4
BAD GUYS DOIN´ WRONG IN THE NIGHT

DEATH WIND

I BELIEVE I WILL DIE
I'LL BE ABLE TO FLY
DON'T YOU CRY FOR ME
JUST LET ME GO

DOCTOR SAYS A WORD
NOTHING I HAVE HEARD
SOMETHING'S WRONG WITH ME
I HAVE TO GO

GOODBYE, MY ANGEL, LET ME FLY
INTO ANOTHER BETTER TIME
OUT OF THE DARKNESS TO THE LIGHT
I SAY GOODBYE
UP IN THE SKY

LET ME THANK YOU FOR THIS
GIVE ME JUST ONE LAST KISS
TAKE CARE OF YOUR LIFE
I'LL THINK OF YOU

SOON I'LL BE OK
DEATH WIND COMES TO STAY
I TAKE ONE LAST BREATH
AND FLY AWAY

GOODBYE, MY ANGEL, HERE I FLY
INTO ANOTHER BETTER TIME
OUT OF THE DARKNESS TO THE LIGHT
I SAY GOODBYE
UP IN THE SKY

DER TAG DER NIEMALS ENDET
(WIRD DER MEINE SEIN)

DER TAG DER NIEMALS ENDET
WIRD DER MEINE SICHER SEIN
DIE HOCHZEIT IN NAHER FERNE
IN DEN EHEHAFEN LAUF ICH EIN

SO SEHR VERLIEBT
IN DEN MANN GANZ IN WEISS
ICH BIN VERLIEBT
IN DEN MANN DER ALLES VON MIR WEISS

KÜSS MICH UND BERÜHR MICH
WENN ICH MEINEN TRAUM ERLEB
LIEB MICH UND VERFÜHR MICH
WENN ES JETZT UM ALLES GEHT
DER TAG DER NIEMALS ENDET
WIRD DER MEINE SICHER SEIN
ICH BIN SO VERLIEBT
ICH BIN DEIN

DER TAG DER NIEMALS ENDET
BILDLICH STELL ICH IHN MIR VOR
ES WIRD SO SCHÖN UND ICH TRÄUME
EINE SO PERFEKTE ILLUSION

DOCH ES IST WAHR
DENN DER PRINZ DER IST DA
ER KNIET VOR MIR
UND NUN, MEIN PRINZ, GEHÖR ICH DIR

KÜSS MICH UND BERÜHR MICH
WENN ICH MEINEN TRAUM ERLEB
LIEB MICH UND VERFÜHR MICH
WENN ES JETZT UM ALLES GEHT
DER TAG DER NIEMALS ENDET
WIRD DER MEINE SICHER SEIN
ICH BIN SO VERLIEBT
ICH BIN DEIN

DERYA

DERYA IS HERE FOR SURE
IN MY HEART AND IN SO MUCH MORE
SHE WAS MY WIFE NEARLY 4 YEARS, SO LONG
BUT OUR LOVE CAN´T CARRY ON
I GAVE YOU ALL I HAD
ALL MY LOVING AND SO MUCH MORE
WE FELT SO FINE HERE JUST LYING IN BED
BUT THE FEELINGS´ NOW TOO LOW

SAY GOODBYE, SAY IT NOW
OVER AND OUT FOR SURE
TIME HAS COME GOING DOWN

DERYA WAS ALL I HAD AND ALL I LOVED
DERYA, I GAVE YOU ALL MY SWEETEST LOVE
YOU ARE THE ONE WHO´S GOING, CAN´T YOU SEE?
I AM IN TEARS, DON´T KNOW WHAT WILL BE

WE PLANNED TO MAKE A CHILD
START A FAMILY AND SOON BE 3
MOVE IN ONE HOUSE WITH OUR NAME ON THE DOOR
OUR LOVE´S NOW HISTORY
DON´T KNOW THE REASON WHY
YOU JUST LEFT ME FOR ALL YOU CAN
TEARS IN MY EYES, I´M SO LONELY INSIDE
YOU JUST HURT YOUR LOVING MAN

SAY GOODNIGHT, TURN AROUND
MAYBE SOME LOVE YOU FOUND
SOMEONE NEW IN YOUR ARMS

YOU WERE JUST ALL I HAD AND ALL I LOVED
DERYA, I GAVE YOU ALL MY SWEETEST LOVE
YOU ARE THE ONE WHO´S GOING, CAN´T YOU SEE?
I AM IN TEARS, DON´T KNOW WHAT WILL BE

ALL ALONE, NO MORE LOVE
WILL IT BE GOOD ENOUGH?
LIVE ALONG ALL MY LIFE

DIE WILDE MARIE

ICH SITZ AN MEINEM TISCH
EIN DRINK BETÄUBT MEINE SORGEN
SEIT ANDREA MICH VERLIESS
BIN ICH LEER
MUSIK ERTÖNT UND DU
BEREITEST MICH VOR AUF MORGEN
TANZT MICH AN UND ICH BIN OFFEN FÜR UNS ZWEI

DIE WILDE MARIE
HOCH OBEN AUF DER BAR
UND MIR WIRD LANGSAM KLAR
DIE WILDE MARIE
DIE MÖCHTE ICH VERFÜHREN
UND DEINE LIEBE SPÜREN

DIE HAARE FEURIG ROT
DIE LIPPEN VERSPRECHEN WAHNSINN
NOCH IST NICHTS GESCHEHEN
DOCH BALD BIN ICH DEIN
ICH ZISCH DEN DRINK HINAB
UND ZWINKER DIR MEINE LIEBE
SPÄTESTENS IN 10 MINUTEN BIST DU MEIN

DIE WILDE MARIE
HOCH OBEN AUF DER BAR
UND MIR WIRD LANGSAM KLAR
DIE WILDE MARIE
DICH MÖCHTE ICH VERFÜHREN
UND DEINE LIEBE SPÜREN

DIGITAL WORLD

NO MORE LOVE, IT IS TRUE
LOVE IS GONE IN THE BLUE

NOW YOU TURN AROUND
PUSH ME TO GROUND
I CAN´T RUN AWAY
AND I HEAR YOU SAY:

NOW DELETE THE THINGS
DIGITAL, THE RINGS
TAKE ´EM BACK FOR SURE
DON´T CALL ME NO MORE!
DIGITAL WORLD
LOST ALL THE PEARLS

FROZEN COLD IS YOUR FACE
NO MORE LOVE IN THIS PLACE

MEMORIES OF OUR LIFE
HURT LIKE A KNIFE
WHY IT HAS TO BE
SUCH BRUTALITY?

HATE IS IN YOUR EYES
I PAY THE PRICE
I CAN´T RUN AWAY
AND I HEAR YOU SAY:

NOW DELETE THE THINGS
DIGITAL, THE RINGS
TAKE ´EM BACK FOR SURE
I DON´T CALL NO MORE
DIGITAL WORLD
LOST ALL THE PEARLS
LOST ALL THE PEARLS

DOCTOR OF LOVE

WHITE NEW YORK CITY LIGHTS
SHOW ME THE WAY
I´VE MISSED SO MANY FLIGHTS
ONE MORE TODAY

TRAVELLING GOOD
ROUND THE WORLD
CALLING MY FRIENDS
AND MY GIRL

I´M JUST A DOCTOR OF LOVE, I FLY
AROUND ALL THE WORLD, I TRY
TO HELP ALL THE BOYS AND THE GIRLS
WOMEN AND MEN, DIFFERENT WORLDS
THE GIRLS ARE HAPPY AND FREE, I SMILE
THEY´RE KISSING THEIR BOYS, I FLY
AROUND ALL THE WORLD AND ABOVE
CAUSE I´M THE SWEET DOCTOR OF LOVE

DARK MUNICH BACKSTREET BOYS
FEELING THE SAME
SWEET PARIS BACKSTREET TOYS
PLAYING THEIR GAME

LOVE ALL AROUND
IN THEIR MINDS
LOOKING FOR LOVE
NO ONE FINDS

I´M JUST A DOCTOR OF LOVE, I FLY
AROUND ALL THE WORLD, I TRY
TO HELP ALL THE BOYS AND THE GIRLS
WOMEN AND MEN, DIFFERENT WORLDS
THE GIRLS ARE HAPPY AND FREE, I SMILE
THEY´RE KISSING THEIR BOYS, I FLY
AROUND ALL THE WORLD AND ABOVE
CAUSE I´M THE SWEET DOCTOR OF LOVE

DOWN THE SHADOWS NEAR THE LIGHT

MY LIFE IS CHANGING NOW FOR SURE
I LEAVE MY LIFE INTO THE BLUE
NO TURNING BACK, I LEAVE BEHIND
I LEAVE BEHIND WHAT´S IN MY MIND

DON´T TURN AROUND, JUST WANNA SEE THE LIGHT
YOU MAKE MY LIFE SO COLOURFUL TONIGHT
IT´S RIGHT I LEFT A PRETTY GIRL FOR YOU
I CUT MY LIFE TO LIVE WITH YOU

HAPPY IN THE SKY AS APOLLO´S RUSHING BY
KISSING NOW WITH YOU JUST MAKES ME FLY
HERE I LIVE ANOTHER LIFE
DOWN THE SHADOWS NEAR THE LIGHT
LEFT BEHIND MY GIRL OF YESTERDAY
HERE I AM AND HERE I WANNA STAY
MY LIFE IS CHANGING NOW
I GUESS I´M BREAKING NOW INTO THE LIGHT

I LEFT BEHIND THE LIFE I HAD
THE PRETTY TIMES AND ALL THE BAD
THE STUPID RULES OF DO AND DON´T
THE SILLY TIMES OF BEING STONED

DON´T TURN AROUND, I WANNA SEE THE LIGHT
YOU MAKE MY LIFE SO BEAUTIFUL TONIGHT
IT´S RIGHT I LEFT MY PRETTY GIRL FOR YOU
I FUCK MY LIFE TO LIVE WITH YOU

HAPPY IN THE SKY AS APOLLO´S RUSHING BY
KISSING NOW WITH YOU JUST MAKES ME FLY
HERE I LIVE ANOTHER LIFE
DOWN THE SHADOWS NEAR THE LIGHT
LEFT BEHIND MY GIRL OF YESTERDAY
HERE I AM AND HERE I WANNA STAY
MY LIFE IS CHANGING NOW
I GUESS I´M BREAKING NOW INTO THE LIGHT

DREAMING OF OUR PARADISE

I WAKE UP, I WAS SLEEPING
NEXT TO YOU IN MY BED
HAND IN HAND GOIN´ NOWHERE
IN THAT DREAM I JUST HAD

I GET UP FOR THIS MORNING
FOR THE DAY NOW AHEAD
EAT MY BREAD, DRINK MY COFFEE
LEAVING YOU IN MY BED

AND WHILE YOU SLEEP I WORK UNTIL THE NIGHT
I´M WORKING HARD UNTIL I SEE THE LIGHT
I SEE YOUR FACE STILL DREAMING OF OUR PARADISE
SO FAR AWAY
I WASH MY FACE AND WASH MY BODY TOO
I BRUSH MY TEETH AND LAY DOWN NEXT TO YOU
AND THEN I DREAM TO BE WITH YOU IN PARADISE
I´M HERE WITH YOU

I WAKE UP, IT´S A NEW DAY
I GET UP, LEAVE MY HOME
WORKING HARD FOR MY MONEY
CUTTING THIS ROLLING STONE

I COME HOME, NOW IT´S MIDNIGHT
THERE YOU ARE IN MY BED
DREAMING DREAMS OF OUR FUTURE
MORE OF TIME I WILL HAVE

I WASH MY FACE AND WASH MY BODY TOO
I BRUSH MY TEETH AND LAY DOWN NEXT TO YOU
AND THEN I DREAM TO BE WITH YOU IN PARADISE
I´M HERE WITH YOU
AND WHILE YOU SLEEP I WORK UNTIL THE NIGHT
I´M WORKING HARD UNTIL I SEE THE LIGHT
I SEE YOUR FACE STILL DREAMING OF OUR PARADISE
SO FAR AWAY

DREAMS HAVE COME TRUE NOW

IS THIS WHAT IT SEEMS?
I´M LOSING CONTROL
YOU´RE ALL OVER ME
IS IT REAL? I CALL
EVERY MOVE, I´M TALL
IS IT A DREAM?
WELL, YOUR KISS IT FEELS LIKE MAGIC
TELL ME IT´S REAL THEN I KNOW

WE´RE IN MY LIVING ROOM
I ROLL THE DICE
WE PLAY STRIP POKER BLUES
THE WORLD IS MINE
OUT OF LINE
DREAMS HAVE COME TRUE NOW, I´M FINE

THE MOMENT WE KISS
THE VERY FIRST TIME
WILL NEVER BE MISSED
IN MY MIND YOU´RE MINE
AND MY WORLD IS FINE
TELL ME FOR SURE
IT IS REAL AND MORE THAN DAYDREAMS
YOU KISS ME TWICE ONCE AGAIN

HERE IN MY LIVING ROOM
I ROLL THE DICE
WE PLAY STRIP POKER BLUES
THE WORLD IS MINE
OUT OF LINE
DREAMS HAVE COME TRUE NOW, I´M FINE

DU, ICH TRÄUME VON DIR

DER MOND IST KLAR UND HELL
GANZ ALLEINE UND ICH TRÄUME
VON UNSEREM GLÜCK ZU ZWEIT
WENN DER WIND DICH ZU MIR WEHT

DIE HOFFNUNG TIEF IN MIR
ALL DIE TRÄNEN LÄNGST VERGEBEN
ICH KANN ES NICHT VERSTEHEN
DASS ICH DICH DAMALS VERLOR
DIESE MELODIE DIE SCHICK ICH DIR JETZT IN DEIN OHR

DU, ICH TRÄUME VON DIR, MÖCHTE DICH JETZT SEHEN
MÖCHTE DICH JETZT BERÜHREN
DIR MEINE LIEBE GESTEHEN
DU, ICH TRÄUME VON DIR SEIT DEM EINEN TAG
ALS ICH SINNLOS UND STUR DIR MEINE LIEBE NAHM

GEBOREN NUR FÜR DICH
DIESE KLARHEIT IST DIE WAHRHEIT
ICH KANN ES ENDLICH SEHEN
UND VERSTEHEN WAS DAMALS WAR

JETZT WEISS ICH WAS ICH WILL
DEINE LIEBE, DIE GEFÜHLE IN MEINEM WARMEN HERZ
DAS NUR SCHLÄGT FÜR DICH UND MICH
DIESE MELODIE DIE IST EINFACH NUR FÜR DICH

DU, ICH TRÄUME VON DIR, MÖCHTE DICH JETZT SEHEN
MÖCHTE DICH JETZT BERÜHREN
DIR MEINE LIEBE GESTEHEN
DU, ICH TRÄUME VON DIR SEIT DEM EINEN TAG
ALS ICH SINNLOS UND STUR DIR MEINE LIEBE NAHM

ICH TRÄUME VON DIR
JA, ICH TRÄUME VON DIR
DIESE HOFFNUNG IN MIR
GIBT MIR KRAFT

EARTHQUAKE INSIDE MY HEAD

SHE TELLS ME EVERY MORNING
HOW SHE LOVES ME IN THE NIGHT
BUT HONESTLY YOUR HANDS ARE FAR AWAY
SHE HIDES UP EVERY MORNING
THINGS I SHOULD HAVE SEEN BEFORE
BUT HONESTLY I´M FOOL ENOUGH TO STAY

SHE´S REALLY PLAYING WITH MY HEART
THE ECHO OF ANOTHER YES OR NO
TAKES ME DOWN, KEEP MOVING ON!

AN EARTHQUAKE RIGHT INSIDE MY HEAD
SHE MAKES ME CRAZY UP INSIDE MY HEAD
A HEATWAVE BLOWS MY MIND AWAY
CONTEMPERATION ON THIS RAINY DAY

SHE SENDS ME SCARY MESSAGES
TOGETHER WITH A KISS
BUT BABY, I DON´T READ THEM ANYMORE
SHE COOKS MY FAVOURITE MEAL
BUT LET ME EAT IT ALL ALONE
SHE´S GETTING SO MUCH STRANGER EVEN MORE

A FIGURE EIGHT IS IN MY HEAD
WHAT SHOULD I DO IF SHE CALLS LOVE AGAIN?
GUESS SHE´S STUCK INSIDE A DREAM

AN EARTHQUAKE RIGHT INSIDE MY HEAD
SHE MAKES ME CRAZY UP INSIDE MY HEAD
A HEATWAVE BLOWS MY MIND AWAY
CONTEMPERATION ON THIS RAINY DAY

EASY JOE

EASY JOE
IS A MAN WHO CAN CHANGE THE WORLD
LET HIM GO
CAUSE HIS PLACE IS NOT WHERE I AM
HE´S A KID WITH MAGICAL HANDS
TAKE HIM OVER

EASY JOE
DOESN´T SPEAK BUT TELLS YOU THE TRUTH
AND HE KNOWS
WHAT WILL BE AHEAD OF HIS TIME
DOESN´T HEAR THE WORDS OF HIS WORLD
UNDERSTANDING

AND HIS EYES MOVING CLOSER NOW
NOT HIS MIND, NOT HIS SOUL
WITH HIS EYES COMING CLOSER NOW
THINGS HE KNOW

EASY JOE TRIES TO SAVE THIS STRATOSPHERE
MIGHTY POWERS NOW ARE NEAR
EASY JOE MAKING SOMETHING VERY REAL
MAGIC POWERS NOW I FEEL, TAKE ME OUT

EASY JOE
DOESN´T SLEEP AND DON´T NEED A GIRL
HE´S ALONE
CAUSE HIS HOME IS FAR, FAR AWAY
WHERE HE COMES FROM NOBODY KNOWS
BUT HE WILL STAY

WITH HIS EYES HE COMMUNICATES
WITH HIS FRIENDS OF THIS TOWN
PLANET EARTH IS IN DANGER SO HELP US, JOE

EASY JOE TRIES TO SAVE THIS STRATOSPHERE
MIGHTY POWERS NOW ARE NEAR
EASY JOE MAKING SOMETHING VERY REAL
MAGIC POWERS NOW I FEEL, TAKE ME HOME

EIN NEUER MORGEN BEGINNT

EIN NEUER MORGEN BRICHT HERAN
ICH WACHE AUF UND SCHAU DICH AN
KENN WEDER NAMEN NOCH DEINE NUMMER
ICH WAR AUS DENN ICH HATTE KUMMER

MEIN SCHÄDEL KLINGELT WIE DIE TÜR
MEIN EX, WAS WILL DENN DER VON MIR?
DIE ROTEN ROSEN SIND MIR SCHNUPPE
ICH BIN KEINESWEGS SEINE ZUCKERPUPPE!

EIN NEUER MORGEN BEGINNT
WER BIST DU IN MEINEM BETT?
ICH SEH DU HAST GAR NICHTS AN
GESTERN ABEND IST EINFACH WEG
UND ALL DER KUMMER UND SCHMERZ
DER MICH QUÄLT JEDE NACHT
IST ENDLICH NICHT MEHR ZU SPÜREN
IN MEINEM HERZ

ICH HATTE EINEN ONE NIGHT STAND
DOCH DEINE AUGEN SIND MIR NICHT FREMD
ES FÜHLT SICH AN ALS WÄREN WIR ZUSAMMEN
SO VERTRAUT UND VERLIEBT HEUT MORGEN

MEIN SCHICKSAL MEINT ES GUT MIT MIR
UND DESHALB BIST JETZT DU BEI MIR
ICH KRIECH ZURÜCK ZU DIR UND FÜHLE
MEIN HERZ SCHLÄGT GANZ WILD
UND ES IST VOLLER LIEBE

EIN NEUER MORGEN BEGINNT
WER BIST DU IN MEINEM BETT?
ICH SEH DU HAST GAR NICHTS AN
GESTERN ABEND IST EINFACH WEG
UND ALL DER KUMMER UND SCHMERZ
DER MICH QUÄLT JEDE NACHT
IST ENDLICH NICHT MEHR ZU SPÜREN
IN MEINEM HERZ

EIN SCHIFF AUF HOHER SEE

EIN SCHIFF AUF HOHER SEE
AUF DEM WEG ZU MIR
MIT NUR EINEM PASSAGIER
15 WOCHEN IST ES HER
UNSER LETZTER KUSS
LANGSAM WIRD ES ZEIT
ICH DENKE NUR AN DICH
SEHE DEIN GESICHT
UND ICH MÖCHTE BEI DIR SEIN
DENN DAS SCHIFF AUF HOHER SEE
ES TUT MIR SO WEH
DASS ICH WARTEN MUSS

UND WENN ICH DICH DANN SEH
AUF DIESEM SCHIFF AUF HOHER SEE
DANN SPRING ICH REIN
EGAL WIE KALT ES IST
DU SPRINGST MIR NACH UND RETTEST MICH
AUF HOHER SEE

ICH WARTE JEDEN TAG
AUF DEN EINEN TAG
WENN DU WIEDER BEI MIR BIST
KANN NICHT SCHLAFEN OHNE DICH
WÄLZ MICH HIN UND HER
TRÄUM DABEI VON DIR
EIN SCHIFF AUF HOHER SEE
DORT AM HORIZONT
JETZT KANN ICH ES WIRKLICH SEHEN
MIT DEM EINEN PASSAGIER
DER MICH WIRKLICH LIEBT
DER MEINE LIEBE SPÜRT

UND WENN ICH DICH JETZT SEH
AUF DIESEM SCHIFF AUF HOHER SEE
DANN SPRING ICH REIN
EGAL WIE KALT ES IST
DU SPRINGST MIR NACH UND RETTEST MICH
AUF HOHER SEE

ELECTRIC TO THE BONE

I´M THE HEAD DEPARTMENT OF TECHNOLOGY
I CAN REPAIR THE HOUSE AND EVEN MORE
IF YOU ASK ME SOMETHING ´BOUT PSYCHOLOGY
I CLOSE THE DOOR

BETTER SHOW ME SOMETHING I CAN FIX IT UP
I USE MY WORK CASE TIL IT´S SAID AND DONE
IF YOU ASK ME NOW TO BE A GENTLE ONE
I´M NEARLY GONE

I´M ELECTRIC TO THE BONE
I PREFER TO WORK ALONE
HANDS OF MAGIC CAN REPAIR
EVERYTHING AND EVERYWHERE

I´M THE HEAD DEPARTMENT OF TECHNOLOGY
I KNOW FOR SURE YOU DON´T BELIEVE IN ME
I´M AFRAID MY HORNY SEXUALITY
IS OUT OF ME

I DON´T CARE TO SEE YOU IN A NEGLIGÉ
AND I DON´T CARE OF BEING CLOSE TO YOU
I HAVE CHANGED MY LIFE INTO A BETTER DAY
THE THINGS I DO

I´M ELECTRIC TO THE BONE
I PREFER TO WORK ALONE
HANDS OF MAGIC CAN REPAIR
EVERYTHING AND EVERYWHERE

EMPTY INSIDE
(THERE'S NO TOMORROW)

7 HOURS ALONE
FAR AWAY FROM THE TRAGIC
LOST MY HOUSE AND MY GIRL
SHE WAS SWEET 17

NOW I FEEL EMPTY INSIDE
NO MORE DAYDREAMS
LOVED HER FOR REAL
THAT'S FOR SURE

THERE'S NO TOMORROW
SCREAMING ALL OUT, I'M ALONE!
I MISS MY BABY
NOW I'M JUST OUT ON MY OWN
EMPTY INSIDE, LOSING MY MIND
AS MY DREAM IS FLYING AWAY
LOSING MY LIFE, LOSING MY DRIVE
AS I PRAY FOR SOME BETTER DAYS

ON THE ROAD ONCE AGAIN
NOTHING LEFT THERE BEHIND ME
SLEEPING ALL BUT ALONE
NO MORE LOVE IN MY HEAD

BUT I KNOW
SEX IS THE ANSWER OF SORROW
MOMENTS OF JOY
NOW I FEEL

THERE'S NO TOMORROW
SCREAMING ALL OUT, I'M ALONE!
I MISS MY BABY
NOW I'M JUST OUT ON MY OWN
EMPTY INSIDE, LOSING MY MIND
AS MY DREAM IS FLYING AWAY
LOSING MY LIFE, LOSING MY DRIVE
AS I PRAY FOR SOME BETTER DAYS

ENGEL IN DER NACHT

SCHÖN BIST DU, ICH TRAU MICH NICHT
DIR DAS ZU GESTEHEN
SCHAU DICH AN UND TRÄUM VON DIR
KANNST DU DAS VERSTEHEN?
STARK WIE EIN WUNDERSCHÖNER TRAUM
KOMM ZU MIR HER IN DIESEN RAUM

WIE EIN ENGEL IN DER NACHT
HALT MICH FEST
WIE EIN ENGEL IN DER NACHT
GANZ ENTSRESST
DU UND ICH, NUR WIR ZWEI GANZ ALLEIN
UND ICH SCHENKE DIR DIE NACHT
HALT DICH FEST
JA, ICH SCHENKE DIR DIE NACHT
KÜSS MICH JETZT
DU UND ICH, NUR WIR ZWEI IM SONNENSCHEIN

WENN DER TAG VORÜBERGEHT
NÄHERT SICH DIE NACHT
KUSCHELZEIT IM ABENDROT
LIEBE IST ENTFACHT
JETZT WO DU WEISST WAS MICH BERÜHRT
DU, DU HAST MICH TOTAL VERFÜHRT

WIE EIN ENGEL IN DER NACHT
HALT MICH FEST
WIE EIN ENGEL IN DER NACHT
GANZ ENTSRESST
DU UND ICH, NUR WIR ZWEI GANZ ALLEIN
UND ICH SCHENKE DIR DIE NACHT
HALT DICH FEST
JA, ICH SCHENKE DIR DIE NACHT
KÜSS MICH JETZT
DU UND ICH, NUR WIR ZWEI IM SONNENSCHEIN

ES IST NICHT MEHR WEIT

ES IST KEIN FRÜHLINGSFEST UND KEIN SOMMERTAG
ICH SCHAU HINAUS
DER ERSTE SCHNEE DER FÄLLT UND DAS LAUB HINAB
ICH BLEIB ZU HAUS
EIN TÄSSCHEN TEE TUT GUT UND DER BALDRIAN
HEY, WO BIST DU?
DU LIEGST IM BETT UND ICH KÜSS DICH SANFT
LIEBLING, SCHLAF GUT

ALL DER KUMMER, ALL DIE TRÄNEN DIE DU SPÜRST
KÜSSE ICH DIR WEG UND DU VERSPÜRST
MEINE GANZE LIEBE NUR FÜR DICH
UND ICH SAGE DIR: ICH LIEBE DICH!
IN DEM ANDEREN LAND WO DU WEILST SEIT GERAUMER ZEIT
DU WIRST WIEDER GLÜCKLICH SEIN MIT MIR
WENN DU WIEDER AUFWACHST HIER BEI MIR
DEINE ZARTEN HÄNDE HALT ICH WARM
ÖFFNE DEINE AUGEN, SCHAU MICH AN
LIEBLING, KOMM ZURÜCK HIER ZU MIR
ES IST NICHT MEHR WEIT

ES WAR EIN FRÜHLINGSFEST, FAST EIN SOMMERTAG
ALS ES GESCHAH
ICH KAM NACH HAUS ZU DIR DOCH DA WARST DU NICHT
ICH SCHLUG ALARM
ICH GING UMS HAUS HERUM UND DANN FAND ICH DICH
WAS WAR GESCHEHEN?
ICH WEISS ES LEIDER BIS HEUTE NICHT
WILL ES VERSTEHEN

ALL DIE FREUDE, ALL DIE LIEBE DIE DU SPÜRST
GIBT DIR KRAFT DAMIT DU NICHT VERLIERST
DU WIRST IMMER GLÜCKLICH SEIN MIT MIR
WENN DU WIEDER AUFWACHST HIER BEI MIR
LIEBLING, KOMM ZURÜCK
DENN DER TRAUM IST NOCH NICHT VORBEI
DEINE ROTEN LIPPEN WILL ICH SPÜREN
UND AUCH DEINE LIEBE NICHT VERLIEREN
WENN DER GROSSE TAG KOMMT BIN ICH DA
UND ICH KÜSS DICH WACH IN MEINEM ARM
LIEBLING, KOMM ZURÜCK HIER ZU MIR
DENN ICH LIEBE DICH

EURESIA

EURESIA, A PRISONER OF MY TIME
THE SUN GOES DOWN
IT´S DANGEROUS WHILE I´M FINE
EURESIA, YOUR TIME IS UP LOSING LINES
THE DAY YOU TURNED AWAY
FROM THE RIGHTFUL SIGNS
TOLD YOU A HUNDRED TIMES
BETTER LEAVE SUSIE ALONE
YOU DIDN´T HEAR AT ALL
NOW WITH YOUR BACK TO THE WALL

CHASE YOU, I´M GONNA CHASE YOU
I´M GONNA BREAK YOU OUT OF THIS TOWN
HATE ME, YOU´RE GONNA HATE ME
I´M GONNA SPIN YOU UP AND AROUND
LEAVE THIS DANGEROUS LAND
AND NEVER COME BACK CAUSE LIFE IS TOO SWEET
RUN AND FOLLOW THE SUN
CAUSE HERE IS THE NIGHT, A DANGEROUS LAND

EURESIA, A PRISONER OF HIS MIND
I TOLD HIM QUITE SOME HUNDRED TIMES
HE IS BLIND
WELL, SUSIE IS A SPECIAL ONE IN MY EYES
SHE KISSED ME ONCE
BUT THEN SHE WAS FULL OF LIES
I DIDN´T GET HER
WELL, I DIDN´T BED HER FOR GOOD
YOU NEVER GET HER
YOU NEVER THINK MAYBE YOU COULD

CHASE YOU, I´M GONNA CHASE YOU
I´M GONNA BREAK YOU OUT OF THIS TOWN
HATE ME, YOU´RE GONNA HATE ME
I´M GONNA SPIN YOU UP AND AROUND
LEAVE THIS DANGEROUS LAND
AND NEVER COME BACK CAUSE LIFE IS TOO SWEET
RUN AND FOLLOW THE SUN
CAUSE HERE IS THE NIGHT, A DANGEROUS LAND

F - I

FINALLY DRIFT AWAY

IN MY CAR OUT TO NOWHERE
I NEED SOME TIME TO DRIFT AWAY
LOSING LIFE, I´VE LOST MY LADY
HER LOVER JOHN ASKED HER TO STAY

BROTHER JOHN WAS MY BROTHER
HE WENT TOO FAR TOO MANY TIMES
BUT THIS TIME HE TOOK MY BABY
HE OVERCROSSED THE LOVING LINES

OH LORD, I´M DRIVING TO THE LIGHT
HELP ME BEFORE I´M GOIN´ WILD
HERE NOW I FINALLY DRIFT AWAY
PRAYING FOR SUCH A BETTER DAY

THEY WERE CLOSE, WE WERE CLOSER
CAN´T BELIEVE YOU DID IT TOO
BROKE MY HEART JUST WITH MY BROTHER
A SILLY TIME AHEAD OF YOU

OH LORD, I´M DRIVING TO THE LIGHT
HELP ME BEFORE I´M GOIN´ WILD
HERE NOW I FINALLY DRIFT AWAY
PRAYING FOR SUCH A BETTER DAY

OH LORD, NOW PARADISE´S PASSING BY
DRIFTING AWAY AND SEARCHING THE LIGHT
WILL I BE LUCKY SOME TIME AGAIN?
CAN I MAKE MYSELF A HAPPY MAN?

FIREBALL IN THE SKY

MONDAY MORNING UP IN THE SKY
THE LUNATIC SUN
EXPLODING UP IN THE BLUE
A FIREFIELD IS BURNING AWAY
SWEET LADY BLUE
OH HEAVENS TRUE
I´M MISSING YOU

A FIRE UP IN THE SKY
HOW CAN IT BE?
NO FANTASY
A FIREBALL IN THE SKY
IT´S OVER NOW
IT´S OVER NOW
THE SUN IS BREAKING AWAY

LOSING LANDS AND LOSING THEIR LIVES
I´M RUNNING AWAY
THE SUN IS BREAKING APART
A WORLD OF FIRE UP IN THE SKY
I CLOSE MY EYES
A BAD SURPRISE
ANOTHER START

A FIRE UP IN THE SKY
HOW CAN IT BE?
NO FANTASY
A FIREBALL IN THE SKY
IT´S OVER NOW
IT´S OVER NOW
THE SUN IS BREAKING AWAY

FLYING TO HEAVEN

BELIEVE
FLYING TO HEAVEN
WITH 947
WITH YOU
WE´RE ON OUR WAY TO THE MOON

I KNOW
ALL OF THE MAGIC
AND ALL OF THE TRAGICAL SHOW
THAT´S WHY WE LEAVE FOR A LAND
FULL OF SUNSHINE AND MORE

THROUGH 20 YEARS OF AGE
THE LIFE ON EARTH FEELS JUST LIKE A CAGE
WITH SHARKS AND DEMONS INSIDE
SO WE MUST GO FOR SURE
WE LEAVE THIS PLACE WE DON´T LIKE NO MORE
AND FLY AWAY TO SALVATIONS BAY TO SOME LIGHT

I´VE TRIED
TO UNDERSTAND THEM
I´VE HAD MANY FRIENDS THEN
ALRIGHT
DIFFERENT I WAS FROM THE START

AND YOU
YOU UNDERSTAND ME
MY SWEET PRETTY CANDY
TONIGHT RIDING TO HEAVEN
WE´RE CLOSING THE DOORS FOR THE FLIGHT

THROUGH 20 YEARS OF AGE
THE LIFE ON EARTH FEELS JUST LIKE A CAGE
WITH SHARKS AND DEMONS INSIDE
SO WE MUST GO FOR SURE
WE LEAVE THIS PLACE WE DON´T LIKE NO MORE
AND FLY AWAY TO SALVATIONS BAY TO SOME LIGHT

FORCE OF TRAGIC

MY TIME IS OVER
I SAY GOODBYE
TO LADY SUNSHINE IN THE SKY
I HAVE TO GO NOW
I TURN AROUND
THE FORCE OF TRAGIC TAKES ME DOWN

HERE I AM ON THE GROUND
AS THE DARK COMES AROUND
DAYS OF PAIN, YEARS SO SAD
COME TO END, I FADE TO BLACK

LEAVING THIS WORLD I KNOW
I´LL BE BETTER EVERYWHERE I GO
NEVER COULD I EXPLAIN ALL MY WOE
NOW I BELIEVE IN YOU
YOU ARE CALLING MY NAME, I DO
FLY AWAY INTO THE SKY UP TO YOU

STRONG FORCE OF TRAGIC
KEPT ME SO DOWN
I WAS A LONER CALLED THE CLOWN
NO PAST, NO FUTURE
WAS THERE TO SEE
A LIFE OF SUNSHINE NOT FOR ME

HERE I AM ON THE GROUND
GOLDEN LIGHT ALL AROUND
ONE MORE LIFE, ONE MORE CHANCE
AND I HOPE I FIND SOME FRIENDS

LEAVING THIS WORLD I KNOW
I´LL BE BETTER EVERYWHERE I GO
NEVER COULD I EXPLAIN ALL MY WOE
NOW I BELIEVE IN YOU
YOU ARE CALLING MY NAME, I DO
FLY AWAY INTO THE SKY UP TO YOU

FOUND MY HOME

HOLY SMOKE
AS I SAY MY LINES TO YOU NOW
FANTASTIC WORDS
THEY WILL NEVER BE THE SAME
A LOT OF PEOPLE IN THE RAIN
HOLY DREAMS
AS I DREAM MY DREAM WITH YOU NOW
FANTASTIC SCENES
THEY WILL NEVER BE THE SAME
A LAND OF SUNSHINE AND NO RAIN

TRY TO SEE THE SUNSHINE
IN A LAND OF ALL IS JOY
UP INTO THIS FUN TIME
HOLY SMOKE UP IN THE SKY
IF IT ENDS A TRAGIC
I CAN TURN AND CARRY HOME
MAYBE IT´S ALL MAGIC
AND I FEEL I FOUND MY HOME

HOLY TIMES
AS I KISS YOU WHERE I KISS YOU
FANTASTIC SIGNS
ALL AROUND YOUR PRETTY FACE
WE´RE GETTING CLOSE THROUGH NIGHTS AND DAYS
HOLY LOVE
AND MY LOVE I GIVE TO YOU NOW
FANTASTIC LOVE
IN THE AIR AND WE´RE LIKE ONE
IT FEELS LIKE SECONDS TO THE SUN

TRY TO SEE THE SUNSHINE
IN A LAND OF ALL IS JOY
UP INTO THIS FUN TIME
HOLY SMOKE UP IN THE SKY
IF IT ENDS A TRAGIC
I CAN TURN AND CARRY HOME
MAYBE IT´S ALL MAGIC
AND I FEEL I FOUND MY HOME

FREIHEIT

AUF MEINEM WEG DES LEBENS
WURDE MIR KLAR
ICH KANN UNENDLICH TRÄUMEN
TROTZ DER GEFAHR
STERBENDER MONUMENTE
PERLEN SO SCHÖN WIE GLAS
ICH SUCH DEN SINN DES LEBENS
FUSS WEG VOM GAS

MEINE FREIHEIT
MEIN GANZES GLÜCK
DEINE TRÄUME
BLICK NICHT ZURÜCK
SCHAU NICHT ZURÜCK

BITTER WAREN ALL DIE TRÄNEN
DIE ICH VERLOR
TRAURIG WAREN DIE MOMENTE
WUSSTEST DU SCHON?
ICH WAR EIN KIND DER STRASSE
KÄMPFTE MICH DANN EMPOR
WEISHEIT UND GLÜCK DES LEBENS
SIND NUN MEIN LOHN

MEINE LIEBE
MEIN GROSSER STOLZ
KEINE LÜGEN
KEIN SCHLECHTES WORT
ZEIG MIR DEN ORT

FROM 1 TO 2

15 1
NOW MY LIFE WILL CHANGE
DAD TO SON
FEELING SOMETHING STRANGE

CREAMY TEARS INTO THE NIGHT
ANGRY FEARS, LOSING THE LIGHT

ME, ME AND YOU
FROM 1 TO 2
NOW MY LIFE WILL CHANGE
FEELING NOTHING BUT STRANGE
BOY, BOY AND GIRL
TWO DIFFERENT WORLDS
I WILL TRY TO FEEL SWEET
THOUGH THIS IS UNREAL

15 1
AS THE TIME WENT BY
ALL ALONE
NEVER HAD TO CRY

ANGRY TEARS PUSH ME TO BED
NO MORE FUN, LYING INSTEAD

ME, ME AND YOU
FROM 1 TO 2
NOW MY LIFE WILL CHANGE
FEELING NOTHING BUT STRANGE
BOY, BOY AND GIRL
TWO DIFFERENT WORLDS
I WILL TRY TO FEEL SWEET
THOUGH THIS IS UNREAL

MAYBE NOW HAPPY AGAIN
GIRL AND BOY, WOMAN AND MAN

FÜR DAS LEBEN, DIE LIEBE UND MEHR

EINSAMKEIT GEHT VORBEI
NACH DER NACHT SCHEINT DIE SONNE
UND ICH FÜHL MICH WIEDER FREI
OHNE DICH

TRAURIGKEIT GEHT VORBEI
NACH DEM LEID KOMMT DIE FREUDE
DIE MIR MEIN LEBEN WIEDER SCHENKT
ALLES NEU, ICH BIN FREI

FÜR DAS LEBEN, DIE LIEBE UND MEHR
FÜR DAS MORGEN
DIESE SINTFLUT VON DEM WAS GESCHAH
LASS ICH LOS
DENN DAS LEBEN, DIE LIEBE UND MEHR
HALTEN MICH GEBORGEN
WIE EIN KIND DAS IMMER LACHT

ANGST UND SCHMERZ GEHEN VORBEI
STUMM UND BLASS DIESE TAGE
DOCH DIE WOLKEN ZIEHEN VORBEI
JEDES MAL

FÜR DAS LEBEN UND MEHR
KÄMPFE ICH DENN ICH LIEBE
UND EINES TAGES FIND ICH DICH
IRGENDWO SOWIESO

ICH BIN FREI
FÜR DAS LEBEN, DIE LIEBE UND MEHR
FÜR DAS MORGEN
DIESE SINTFLUT VON DEM WAS GESCHAH
LASS ICH LOS
DENN DAS LEBEN, DIE LIEBE UND MEHR
HALTEN MICH GEBORGEN
WIE EIN KIND DAS IMMER LACHT

GIVE ME THE KISS

HOW MANY TIMES
HOW MANY LIVES
WILL IT TAKE FOR ME TO DIE?

HIGH AND ABOVE
UP TO SOME LOVE
DON´T WANNA COME BACK AGAIN

NO, I SAY NO TO HATE AND LIES
I´M ON MY WAY TO PARADISE
LOVE IS THE REASON FOR ALL THIS
COME, BUTTERFLY, GIVE ME THE KISS

SO MANY DAYS
HUNDREDS OF WAYS
I TRIED TO SHINE AND BE STRONG

I´VE TO ADMIT
CAN´T LEAVE THIS SHIT
IT´S TIME TO MOVE ON FOR SURE

NO, I SAY NO TO HATE AND LIES
I´M ON MY WAY TO PARADISE
LOVE IS THE REASON FOR ALL THIS
COME, BUTTERFLY, GIVE ME THE KISS

GREET BARRIER REEF
(A SUMMER OF LOVE)

BROWN, BROWN IS THE SKY
EARLY BIRDS IN THE MORNING
I DON'T WANNA CRY
LIKE A PAIR LEAVING BEHIND
ALL WHAT'S IN THEIR MIND

BROWN IS THE SKY AS ALWAYS
WHEN THE WAVES EAT THE SHORE
SEXY, THE PRETTY LADY, I WANT MORE

GREAT BARRIER REEF
A SUMMER OF LOVE
SPECTACULAR SPEACH
A FACE OF LOVE
GREAT BARRIER REEF
A FANTASY LAND
I NEED A FRIEND

BLUE, BLUE IS THE MOON
AND THE STARS SEEM SO LONELY
I FOLLOW THE TUNE
SILVER BIRDS UP IN THE SKY
AS THE SUN GOES BY

HOT AND AGAIN SO COLD NOW
IN MY MIND, IN MY HEAD
SEXY, THE PRETTY LADY, IN MY BED

GREAT BARRIER REEF
A SUMMER OF LOVE
SPECTACULAR SPEACH
A FACE OF LOVE
GREAT BARRIER REEF
A FANTASY LAND
I FOUND A FRIEND

ONE MORE GAME
ONE MORE NAME

HAPPY LITTLE STAN

HAPPY LITTLE SUNSHINE, HAPPY LITTLE TUNE
HAPPY LITTLE MAGIC, HAPPY LITTLE MOON
HAPPY LITTLE WOMAN, HAPPY LITTLE MAN
HAPPY LITTLE DAYDREAMS, HAPPY LITTLE STAN

HAPPY LITTLE WORKFLOW, HAPPY LITTLE LIFE
HAPPY LITTLE JOURNEY, HAPPY LITTLE DIVE
HAPPY LITTLE STRANGER, HAPPY LITTLE FRIENDS
HAPPY LITTLE LOVE GAME, HAPPY LITTLE STAN

700 WORDINGS, 700 RHYMES
STAN IS HERE TO MAKE YOU HAPPY
700 TIMES
700 KISSES, 700 SMILES
STAN IS HERE TO MAKE YOU HAPPY
700 TIMES

HAPPY LITTLE SISTER, HAPPY LITTLE JOB
HAPPY LITTLE TINDER, HAPPY LITTLE DOG
HAPPY LITTLE BARFIGHT, HAPPY LITTLE VAN
HAPPY LITTLE SHOWER, HAPPY LITTLE STAN

HAPPY LITTLE DING DONG, HAPPY LITTLE STREET
HAPPY LITTLE HOURS, HAPPY LITTLE CHEAT
HAPPY LITTLE EARRING, HAPPY LITTLE BAND
HAPPY LITTLE MUSIC, HAPPY LITTLE STAN

700 WORDINGS, 700 RHYMES
STAN IS HERE TO MAKE YOU HAPPY
700 TIMES
700 KISSES, 700 SMILES
STAN IS HERE TO MAKE YOU HAPPY
700 TIMES

HEY, I´M IN LOVE

I TURN THE RADIO ON TO HEAR YOU
I READ YOUR LETTERS EVERY DAY
YOU´RE FAR AWAY NOW, CAN YOU HEAR ME?
SOME WORDS OF LOVE AND MORE TO SAY

WHEN THINGS GOT DIZZY YOU WERE LEAVING
A SPECIAL JOB IN SAN JOSE
I´M STILL ALONE AND STILL I´M WAITING
FOR ANY DAY YOU COME AGAIN

HEY, I´M IN LOVE
HEY, I´M IN LOVE
HEY, I´M IN LOVE
HEY, I´M IN LOVE

I SEND YOU E-MAILS MORE THAN THOUSANDS
YOU HARDLY ANSWER, THERE´S NO TIME
I TRY TO CALL YOU, THERE´S NOBODY
I KNOW YOUR JOB IS ON THE LINE

1 YEAR HAS GONE NOW I´M SO HUNGRY
TO GET YOU BACK AND KISS YOUR HEAD
TOMORROW MORNING MAYBE NEXT WEEK
I PRAY TO GOD YOU´RE BACK AGAIN

HEY, I´M IN LOVE
HEY, I´M IN LOVE
HEY, I´M IN LOVE
HEY, I´M IN LOVE

HOCH & HÖHER

DER FRÜHLING UND DER SOMMER
DIE SONNE SO SCHÖN
ICH GEH SO GERN AUF DIE BERGE
MIT MAMA UND PAPA
WIR WANDERN SO HOCH
DIE BERGLUFT MACHT UNS LUSTIG
UND SO FROH

DORT WO BLUMEN SPRIESSEN
SEHEN WIR DAS PARADIES
DORT WO DIE WOLKEN VERFLIEGEN
WERDEN MEINE TRÄUME WAHR

HOCH UND HÖHER
ICH STEIG HINAUF
BIS ZU DER SPITZE WIEDER
HOCH UND HÖHER
ICH FLIEG HINAUF
BIS DASS DER BERG MICH KÜSST

MAMA, DU BIST BEI MIR
DU PASST AUF MICH AUF
DASS MIR REIN GAR NICHTS PASSIEREN KANN
UND PAPA, DU WARTEST
AM GIPFEL AUF MICH
ZUSAMMEN SCHAUEN WIR DANN HINEIN INS LICHT

DORT WO TIERE SPIELEN
SEHEN WIR DAS PARADIES
WENN ICH DEN HIMMEL BERÜHRE
SIND MEINE TRÄUME WAHR

HOCH UND HÖHER
ICH STEIG HINAUF
BIS ZU DER SPITZE WIEDER
HOCH UND HÖHER
ICH FLIEG HINAUF
BIS DASS DER BERG MICH KÜSST

HOME OF LOVIN´

I´M IN LOVE
I WON´T LEAVE
YOU´RE MY SPECIAL ONE
YOU´RE MY DREAM
I FOUND THE TRUTH
FOUND MY LOVE
WE´LL STAY TOGETHER
THROUGH GOOD AND ROUGH

BUILD A HOME OF LOVIN´ JUST FOR YOU
MAKE SOME BREAKFAST EVERY MORNING TOO
I KISS YOU DAYS AND NIGHTS ARE PASSING BY

BUY RED ROSES EVERY DAY FOR YOU
GO TO WORK FOR SWEET VACATION TOO
I´LL MAKE OUR LIFE SO GOOD
WE TOUCH THE SKY

I WAKE UP
WITH A SMILE
WITH A BEAUTY ONE
HERE I FLY
I FOUND THE LOVE
AND THE KEY
WILL YOU FOREVER
JUST STAY WITH ME?

BUILD A HOME OF LOVIN´ JUST FOR YOU
MAKE SOME BREAKFAST EVERY MORNING TOO
I KISS YOU DAYS AND NIGHTS ARE PASSING BY

BUY RED ROSES EVERY DAY FOR YOU
GO TO WORK FOR SWEET VACATION TOO
I´LL MAKE OUR LIFE SO GOOD
WE TOUCH THE SKY

HONIGMOND

HONIGMOND
DEINE TRÄNEN IN MEINER HAND
SPIELEN EIN LIED
DIESE EINE MELODIE

KOMM, HALT MICH FEST
WENN DER WIND SO STÜRMISCH WEHT
WENN DIE PANIKLEITER STEHT
KOMM UND HALT MICH FEST
HONIGMOND

ICH BIN SO ALLEIN OHNE DICH
HONIGMOND, SCHENK MIR DIE LIEBE
BIST DU AUCH SO EINSAM OHNE MICH?
OHNE DICH IST ALLES GRAU
UND DURCH DIESEN STURM WILL ICH GEHEN
WIE EIN FELSEN IN DER BRANDUNG
MÖCHTE ALLE LÄNDER MIT DIR SEHEN
MEIN HONIGMOND

HONIGMOND
HAND IN HAND MIT DIR
DURCH DIE WELT UND ZURÜCK
VOLLER LIEBE, VOLLER GLÜCK

KOMM, HALT MICH FEST
WENN DIE ERDE MÄCHTIG BEBT
WENN DIE LETZTE STUNDE SCHLÄGT
DANN BIST DU BEI MIR
HONIGMOND

ICH BIN SO ALLEIN OHNE DICH
HONIGMOND, SCHENK MIR DIE LIEBE
BIST DU AUCH SO EINSAM OHNE MICH?
OHNE DICH IST ALLES GRAU
UND DURCH DIESEN STURM WILL ICH GEHEN
WIE EIN FELSEN IN DER BRANDUNG
MÖCHTE ALLE LÄNDER MIT DIR SEHEN
MEIN HONIGMOND

I DIE IN PAIN

GOODBYE, MY LOVE
I WILL SEE YOU HIGH ABOVE
IT ENDS IN PAIN
AND I FEEL IT´S SUCH A SHAME

I CLOSE THE DOOR
DRINK SO MUCH MORE
THEN CLOSE MY EYES, I AM FREE

I DIE IN PAIN
FEELING SO WEAK
IT´S NOT A GAME
I DIE ALONG
THINKING OF YOU
SINGING THIS SONG
LORD, HERE I COME
OVER AND DONE

WE SHARED A LOVE
SO MUCH DEEPER THAN A SEA
OUR SPECIAL LOVE
MADE US NEVER PART TIL WE

CHANGED, IT WAS YOU
OUT OF THE BLUE
YOU STROLLED AWAY, SOMEONE NEW

I DIE IN PAIN
FEELING SO WEAK
IT´S NOT A GAME
I DIE ALONG
THINKING OF YOU
SINGING THIS SONG
LORD, HERE I COME
OVER AND DONE

I HAD 69

A 69 WAS IN MY HOUSE
I NEVER THOUGHT THIS HAPPENED TO ME
SHE WAS A BEAUTY ONE NOT IN DISGUISE
AND TAUGHT ME THINGS THAT MADE MY BODY FLY

I WAS SO HAPPY WITH HER SMILE
THIS SEXY LADY NOW WAS MINE
I TURNED AROUND BUT SHE WAS AWAY

I HAD 69
NOW I´M LONELY ALL THE TIME
WAS SHE REALLY THERE?
IN MY ARMS AND OUT OF DESPERATION
I BELIEVE IN YOU
BETTER TELL ME THAT IT´S TRUE
I´M WAITING FOR THE DAY
YOU COME BACK INTO MY ARMS
AND THERE YOU´LL STAY

A 69 WAS IN MY ROOM
SHE TAUGHT ME THINGS I COULDN´T BELIEVE
IT WAS ELECTRIFYING TO SEE HER COME
AND IN THE END SHE SMILED TO LET ME GO

BUT WHEN I CAME BACK INTO LIFE
I COULDN´T SEE HER WITH MY EYES
I TURNED AROUND AND SHE WAS AWAY

I HAD 69
NOW I´M LONELY ALL THE TIME
WAS SHE REALLY THERE?
IN MY ARMS AND OUT OF DESPERATION
I BELIEVE IN YOU
BETTER TELL ME THAT IT´S TRUE
I´M WAITING FOR THE DAY
YOU COME BACK INTO MY ARMS
AND THERE YOU´LL STAY

I HELPED HER UP

I´M JUST A MAN
PLEASE FORGIVE ME, MY DEAR
SHE´S FAR AWAY
IT WAS JUST ONE LAST BEER
SORRY, MY DEAR, I WAS WRONG

SHE RODE A BIKE
AND BEFORE I COULD STOP
I HIT HER STRAIGHT
AND HER CUTE PRETTY BOD
YES, SHE WAS HOT
TOOK THE FALL

I HELPED HER UP
AND HER EYES
WERE FULL OF TEARS
BUT NO LIES
WE DROVE AWAY
TO HER ROOM
I SAID GOODBYE
VERY SOON

DON´T GET ME WRONG
THERE´S AN ANGEL IN ME
I HAD TO HELP
HAD TO TAKE CARE OF SHE
NOW YOU CAN SEE
YOU WERE WRONG

I HELPED HER UP
AND HER EYES
WERE FULL OF TEARS
BUT NO LIES
WE DROVE AWAY
TO HER ROOM
I SAID GOODBYE
VERY SOON

I KNOW BUT

I KNOW YOU CAN CARRY ME HOME
BUT I THINK OF BEING ALONE
OUR LOVE HAS CHANGED
I´M OUT ON MY OWN

I KNOW YOU CAN MARRY ME TWICE
BUT YOU LOST THE SMILE IN YOUR EYES
LET´S BE HONEST NOW
THERE´RE SO MANY GUYS

SO PACK YOUR BAGS AND DRIFT AWAY
OUR LOVE IS OVER NOW I SAY
SADNESS I FEEL BUT THIS IS OK
NOW I PREFER TO STAY ALONE
I´M BETTER LIVING ON MY OWN
A HOLIDAY TIME I FEEL IS MINE

I KNOW YOU CAN LIVE IN MY HOUSE
BUT I HAVE TO SHUT UP MY MOUTH
CAN´T GO ON TO LIVE
A PRISONER´S LIFE

I KNOW YOU CAN GIVE ME A HIGH
BUT YOU MORE OF MAKING ME CRY
IT´S NOT GOOD ENOUGH
JUST MAKING ME FLY

SO PACK YOUR BAGS AND DRIFT AWAY
OUR LOVE IS OVER NOW I SAY
SADNESS I FEEL BUT THIS IS OK
NOW I PREFER TO STAY ALONE
I´M BETTER LIVING ON MY OWN
A HOLIDAY TIME I FEEL IS MINE

I PACK AND RUN AWAY

OUR LOVE IS OVER NOW, I SAY
THE TIME HAS COME FOR ME
I RUN AWAY
THE REASON I GO
IF YOU ASK ME WHY

YOU CHANGED FROM LOVELY, CAN´T YOU SEE?
INTO A MONSTER
AND YOU´RE AFTER ME
A DEVIL YOU ARE
A ONE IN DISGUISE

AND SO I PACK AND RUN AWAY
BEFORE IT´S TOO LATE
AND YOU BROKE MY WILL TO GO
WITH SWEET MADELAINE I WANNA STAY
SHE LOVES ME FOR REAL
AND OPENS HER ARMS FOR ME I KNOW

I TRIED TO BE THE PERFECT ONE
WAS THERE FOR YOU
YOUR GIRL, YOUR DOG AND SON
WAS DOIN´ IT ALL
TO MAKE YOU FEEL RIGHT

I PAID THE HOUSE YOU HAD TO PAY
YOU SMILED WHILE I JUST
WORKED MY LIFE AWAY
I DID IT FOR YOU
ALL DAY AND ALL NIGHT

AND SO I PACK AND RUN AWAY
BEFORE IT´S TOO LATE
AND YOU BROKE MY WILL TO GO
WITH SWEET MADELAINE I WANNA STAY
SHE LOVES ME FOR REAL
AND OPENS HER ARMS FOR ME I KNOW

I SEE YOU FLY

DYING NEXT TO YOU
FLYING OVER YOU
UP INTO THE BLUE AND FAR AWAY
ANGEL 99, ANGEL 69
ANGEL 49 TAKE CARE OF YOU

I TURN AROUND AND START TO CRY
I WONDER WHY, I WONDER WHY
I FEEL THE DANGER OF THE SKY
AS SCARY CLOUDS ARE PASSING BY

AND IN THE WORLD OF YOU AND I
I SEE YOU FLY, I SEE YOU FLY
AND IN MY WORLD OF ENDLESS HOPE
I USE THIS BLUE KALEIDOSCOPE

FALLING NEXT TO YOU
FLYING OVER YOU
IS IT JUST A DREAM OR IS IT REAL?
ANGEL 41, ANGEL 61
ANGEL 91 TAKE CARE OF YOU

I RUN AWAY INTO THE NIGHT
TO SEE THE LIGHT, TO SEE THE LIGHT
WHAT´S WRONG AND REAL I HAVE TO KNOW
I BETTER GO, YOU BETTER GO

AND IN THE WORLD OF YOU AND I
I SEE YOU FLY, I SEE YOU FLY
AND IN MY WORLD OF ENDLESS HOPE
I USE THIS BLUE KALEIDOSCOPE

I TAKE MY HEART BACK FROM YOU

TELL ME, SHOW ME
TELL ME ALL ABOUT MY HEART
BROKEN, SPOKEN
BROKEN WORDS DRIFT ME APART

SAD ABOUT THE THINGS YOU SAID
BAD, I´M LYING IN MY BED
HATRED CONSEQUENCE
WHILE IT WAS A ROMANCE

I TAKE MY HEART BACK FROM YOU
DON´T DESERVE MY SEXY LOVE
TAKE BACK MY HEART
WITH THE POWERS FROM ABOVE
I TAKE MY HEART BACK FROM YOU
ARE A CREEPY YELLOW FLY
TAKE BACK MY HEART
WITH THE FORCE OF MY DESIRE

ONE DAY, SOME DAY
I WILL FIND A BETTER LOVE
HONEY, MONEY
ONLY CARE ABOUT YOURSELF

SAD ABOUT THE WAY IT ENDS
FRIENDS, I THINK WE WON´T BE FRIENDS
UGLY CONSEQUENCE
OUT OF SUCH A ROMANCE

I TAKE MY HEART BACK FROM YOU
DON´T DESERVE MY SEXY LOVE
TAKE BACK MY HEART
WITH THE POWERS FROM ABOVE
I TAKE MY HEART BACK FROM YOU
ARE A CREEPY YELLOW FLY
TAKE BACK MY HEART
WITH THE FORCE OF MY DESIRE

I´M COMING HOME

THROUGH RAIN AND HAILSTONES I DRIVE
MAKING A BREAK ROUND ABOUT 10
HAVE A DRINK AND SOME DROPS
READING THE PAPER, CALLING A FRIEND
I´M COMING HOME THIS TIME AND AGAIN
COMING HOME

WORKING A LOT 300 DAYS
LIVING IN NOWHERE
DON´T KNOW THE PLACE
TRAVELLING FORTH AND BACK THE LAND
LOSING MY FAMILY AND MY FRIENDS
NOW COMING HOME
I´M COMING HOME

I´M A WORKER, ALRIGHT, WORK FOR A DAY
HARD WORKING LIFE
EVERY NIGHT AFTER WORK
DRINKING SOME WHISKY, DRINKING MY BEER
GOING TO SLEEP AND FIGHTING MY FEAR
LOSING ALL

WORKING A LOT 300 DAYS
LIVING IN NOWHERE
DON´T KNOW THE PLACE
TRAVELLING FORTH AND BACK THE LAND
LOSING MY FAMILY AND MY FRIENDS
NOW COMING HOME
I´M COMING HOME
I´M COMING HOME
I´M COMING HOME

I´M LOSING LOVE

REASON IS DOWN, SHAKING MY HEAD
WHISKY I DRINK HERE IN MY BED
SEEING YOUR FACE DOWN ON THE WALL
TEARS IN MY EYES, I´M SO ALONE
WHY DID YOU GO?
WHY DID YOU GO?

TOUCHING MY SKIN, STROKING MY LEGS
DREAMING OF PURE INTENSIVE SEX
WE HAD ALL DAYS, WE HAD ALL NIGHTS
THINKING OF WARM DECEMBER NIGHTS
LOOKING FOR YOU
WAITING FOR YOU

NOWHERE IN TIME I´M LOSING LOVE
WHY DID YOU GO? YOU KILLED MY LOVE
UGLY THE WORDS YOU SAID TO ME SO EASILY
NOWHERE IS NEAR, I´VE LOST MY LOVE
NOWHERE IS HERE, THERE´S NO MORE LOVE
TEARDROPS OF PAIN, IT´S NOT A GAME
YOU KILLED MY LOVE

BODIES SO CLOSE, HOLDING YOU TIGHT
MEMORIES OF LOVE THEY REUNITE
DREAMING A DREAM, FEELING SO REAL
FEELING SO GOOD BUT NOW I FEEL
IT´S JUST A DREAM
IT´S JUST MY DREAM

NOWHERE IN TIME I´M LOSING LOVE
WHY DID YOU GO? YOU KILLED MY LOVE
UGLY THE WORDS YOU SAID TO ME SO EASILY
NOWHERE IS NEAR, I´VE LOST MY LOVE
NOWHERE IS HERE, THERE´S NO MORE LOVE
TEARDROPS OF PAIN, IT´S NOT A GAME
YOU KILLED MY LOVE

I´M MISSING YOU

I THINK OF YOU
AND OUR TIME
WE THOUGHT OUR LOVE
WOULD CROSS THE LINE
I SEE YOUR FACE
STILL IN MY DREAMS
I FEEL YOUR TOUCH
INSIDE MY JEANS

ALL THE MEMORIES SEEM SO FAR AWAY
ALL THE LAUGHING AND THE PRETTY DAYS
I´M MISSING YOU

ON THE DAY I HAVE TO DIE
YOU SEE ME FLY UP THERE TO YOU AGAIN
I KNOW YOU´RE NOT SO FAR AWAY
AND ON THAT DAY I´M KISSING YOU AGAIN

I THINK OF YOU
10 YEARS AGO
THIS DREADED CAR
I MISS YOU SO
AND SINCE THAT DAY
I´M IN A MESS
I LIVE ALONE
I TRY MY BEST

ALL THE DAYS AND ALL THE NIGHTS WITH YOU
ALL THE FUN AND ALL THE LOVING TOO
I´M MISSING YOU

ON THE DAY I HAVE TO DIE
YOU SEE ME FLY UP THERE TO YOU AGAIN
I KNOW YOU´RE NOT SO FAR AWAY
AND ON THAT DAY I´M KISSING YOU AGAIN

ICH LIEBE DICH

GEHT DIE SONNE UNTER
WIRD ES DUNKLER RUNDHERUM
BIS AUF DEINE AUGEN
DIE DA FUNKELN SCHÖN UND JUNG

ENDLOS LANGE LIEDER
UND GESCHICHTEN SIE ERZÄHLEN
ICH HÖR GERNE ZU
DENN SIE SIND WIRKLICH WUNDERSCHÖN
SO SCHÖN WIE DU

UND WIEDER EIN TAG DU UND ICH
UND DU WEISST: ICH LIEBE DICH
KOMMT DIE NACHT
KOMM ICH NOCH NÄHER RAN AN DICH
DIE HÄNDE SO ZART WIE DEIN HAAR
DEINE AUGEN STERNENKLAR
KOMMT DER MOND HINAUS
BIN ICH IN DEINEM HAUS

AUF DEN MALEDIVEN
TIEF IM SÜDEN, IN PARIS
ICH ZEIG DIR DIE LIEDER
UND DAS STERNENPARADIES

KONZIPIERTE LIEDER
UND GESCHICHTEN NUR FÜR DICH
KOMM IN MEINE ARME
DENN DU WEISST: ICH LIEBE DICH
WIR SCHLAFEN EIN

UND WIEDER EIN TAG DU UND ICH
UND DU WEISST: ICH LIEBE DICH
KOMMT DIE NACHT
KOMM ICH NOCH NÄHER RAN AN DICH
DIE HÄNDE SO ZART WIE DEIN HAAR
DEINE AUGEN STERNENKLAR
KOMMT DER MOND HINAUS
BIN ICH IN DEINEM HAUS

J - L

JO, JACKY, JANE

A-HUNDRED PEOPLE SIT ALONG, NOT SPEAKING A WORD
THEY´RE WAITING FOR THEIR TRAIN
IT´S LATE LIKE A BIRD
THEIR FACES IN UGLINESS, OLD PEOPLE I SEE
I FEEL THEY GO CRAZY NOW
DON´T KNOW WHAT WILL BE

STILL WAITING, AGGRESSIVE NOW
THEY DON´T GIVE A DAMN
RED FACES AND SCREAMING WORDS
DON´T KNOW WHO I AM
I´M WAITING FOREVER NOW, IT´S DARKNESS OUTSIDE
A SHAME, I AM SO CONFUSED
I WANT TAKE A RIDE

JO, JACKY, JANE, I WILL BE LATE
PLEASE, PLEASE FORGIVE ME
I´M TOO LATE FOR OUR DATE
JO, JACKY, JANE, WHAT CAN I SAY?
SEE NOW THIS MESS HAVE COME MY WAY NOW TODAY

A-THOUSAND PEOPLE SIT ALONG
I´M SITTING THE SAME
DEMONS IN THE AIR I SEE SO BLACK AND AGAIN
THEIR FACES IN UGLINESS, I´M SHAKING IN FEAR
TRAIN PLEASE SHOULD COME NOW SOON
NOW, NOT IN ONE YEAR

JO, JACKY, JANE, I WILL BE LATE
PLEASE, PLEASE FORGIVE ME
I´M TOO LATE FOR OUR DATE
JO, JACKY, JANE, WHAT CAN I SAY?
SEE NOW THIS MESS HAVE COME MY WAY NOW TODAY

FINALLY I SEE AND I HEAR
TRAIN IS COMING NEAR
FINALLY SOME JOY IN THE AIR
IN THE TRAIN AND EVERYWHERE

JOHNNY AND JILL WE ARE

TURN RIGHT AND FOLLOW THE EASY WAY
TURN LEFT AND LEAVE ME ALONE
WELL, IT´S TIME TO UNDERSTAND
I´M MORE TO YOU THAN A FRIEND
HANDS UP TO THE MORNING LIGHT

GET UP AND BRING ME A MORNING DRINK
LAY DOWN AND DO WHAT I WANT
ALL I WANT IS JUST A SMILE
YOU MAKE MY LIVING WORTHWHILE
HANDS DOWN FOR ANOTHER NIGHT

JOHNNY AND JILL WE ARE
OWN A HOUSE, A POOL AND A CAR
MARRIED WE ARE FOR SURE
BUT THE TIME HAS DAMAGED THE DOOR
HATE AND GREED HAVE CHANGED OUR QUALITY LIFE
THOUGH WE TRY TO LOVE EACH OTHER TONIGHT

I THINK I´VE TOLD YOU A HUNDRED TIMES
JUST THEN TO LET ME ALONE
WHEN I NEED A TIME OF BREAK
BUT YOU JUST SHIT ON MY CAKE
DON´T YOU UNDERSTAND MY HEART?

BUT THIS IS SOMETHING I WANNA SAY
I´M STILL SO HAPPY WITH YOU
ALL THE YEARS AND ALL THE LINES
WE WENT THROUGH DIFFERENT TIMES
BETTER NOT TO DRIFT APART

JOHNNY AND JILL WE ARE
OWN A HOUSE, A POOL AND A CAR
MARRIED WE ARE FOR SURE
BUT THE TIME HAS DAMAGED THE DOOR
HATE AND GREED HAVE CHANGED OUR QUALITY LIFE
THOUGH WE TRY TO LOVE EACH OTHER TONIGHT

JULIET, A GHOST I SEE

I BELIEVE I´M IN A MESS
RIGHT OR WRONG? PLEASE TAKE A GUESS
HOLY SMOKE LIKE CRYSTAL METH
ONE MORE TIME AND ONE MORE BREATH

JULIET
A GHOST I SEE
10 FEET TALL AWAY FROM ME
SCARY EYES LIKE MR. T
CHARLIE SHEEN IS HAUNTING ME
WILL I FALL OR WILL I DIE?
IN MY CHAIR I START TO CRY
HOLY SHIT, IT SEEMS THE END
CLOSE MY EYES AND UNDERSTAND

WHEN I WAKE I TRY TO SMILE
AND I WALK ANOTHER MILE
SUN GOES DOWN, I START TO CRY
ONE MORE WINE AND ONE MORE LIE

JULIET
MY TIME HAS COME
SAY GOODBYE BEFORE THE JUMP
RIGHT INTO ANOTHER LIFE
IN A TIME I FEEL ALRIGHT
IS IT TRUE WHAT PEOPLE SAY?
WHEN I GO YOU TURN AWAY
THOUGH I DIE THE WORLD GOES ON
AS I FEEL I´M LOSING STRONG

KEEP IT GOING STRONG

I CARRY ON
YOU KEEP IT STRONG

SO MANY PAIRS IN THIS WORLD
LIVING ALONG SO DISTURBED
FREEDOM IS NOT WHAT THEY KNOW

WE ARE SO DIFFERENT NOW
WE TRY TO UNDERSTAND
ALL OF OUR PROBLEMS
AND THE THINGS WE DON´T UNDERSTAND
WE CARRY ON FOR SURE
WE KEEP IT GOING STRONG
WE MAKE IT DIFFERENT
THAN THE OTHERS DOING SO WRONG
CARRY ON

WE CARRY ON
WE KEEP IT STRONG

AFTER A COUPLE OF YEARS
AFTER A COUPLE OF TEARS
FREEDOM IS ALL WHAT WE KNOW

WE ARE SO DIFFERENT NOW
WE TRY TO UNDERSTAND
ALL OF OUR PROBLEMS
AND THE THINGS WE DON´T UNDERSTAND
WE CARRY ON FOR SURE
WE KEEP IT GOING STRONG
WE MAKE IT DIFFERENT
THAN THE OTHERS DOING SO WRONG
KEEP IT STRONG

KILLER QUEEN

ANOTHER NIGHT WHITE SNOW OUTSIDE
AND I´M AT HOME ALONE AND CRY
THE SWORD IS BLEEDING RED I SEE, IT HAD TO BE
HE WENT TOO FAR AND HAD TO DIE

AND IN MY LITTLE HOUSE UPON THAT LONESOME HILL
I WASH MY HANDS, I WASH MY FACE
THE BLOODY GHOST CAME BACK
INSPIRED NOW THE KILLER QUEEN IN MANY WAYS

AS THE SNOW IS FALLING DOWN
UP FROM THE SKY
LADY LUCK JUST CHANGED HER MIND
HE HAD TO DIE
HE´S NOT THE ONLY ONE FOR SURE
IN THIS OLD HOUSE
I´M THE KILLER QUEEN
AND KILL WITH HANDS AND MOUTH

ANOTHER DAY THE SKY IS GREY
IT OVERCAME ME ONCE AGAIN
ANOTHER SIMPLE BLOKE HE WAS, A FRIENDY ONE
BUT AFTER WE HAD OUR FUN

I TOOK CONTROL OF ALL THE DEADLY WEAPONS I
HAVE IN MY HOUSE AND IN MY ROOM
THE BLOODY BLOOD IS STILL SO FRESH
AND WHILE I LAUGH AND CRY I FEEL THE DOOM

AS THE SNOW IS FALLING DOWN
UP FROM THE SKY
LADY LUCK JUST CHANGED HER MIND
HE HAD TO DIE
HE´S NOT THE ONLY ONE FOR SURE
IN THIS OLD HOUSE
I´M THE KILLER QUEEN
AND KILL WITH HANDS AND MOUTH

LAHAMI BAY

LAHAMI IS MY HAPPY PLACE
THE EGYPT LAND OF RAMSES KING
I´VE BEEN THERE ROUND A DOZEN TIMES
THE PERFECT THING

DUGONGS AND STINGRAYS MAKE ME SMILE
DOWN IN THE BLUE NOT IN THE SKY
THERE´S SUNSHINE ALL AROUND THE CLOCK
DON´T ASK ME WHY

LET´S FLY TO LAHAMI BAY
WHERE DREAMS COME TRUE I DREAM AWAY
A PARADISE NOT KNOWN BY THE LAGOS WORLD
UP TO THIS DAY
LET´S RIDE TO LAHAMI BAY
WHERE DOLPHINS FLY AND TURTLES PLAY
HERE I FORGET MY LIFE AS A WORKING MAN
LAHAMI BAY

LAHAMI IS MY ATTITUDE
A COCKTAIL COOL RIGHT IN THE POOL
I SEE A MAN AFRAID OF ICE
HE´S SUCH A FOOL

THE FOOD IS SO DELICIOUS LIKE
I EAT ALL DAY AND SWIM AWAY
I ASK YOU THIS AS ROMEO
YOU HEAR ME SAY:

LET´S FLY TO LAHAMI BAY
WHERE DREAMS COME TRUE WE DREAM AWAY
A PARADISE NOT KNOWN BY THE LAGOS WORLD
UP TO THIS DAY
LET´S RIDE TO LAHAMI BAY
WHERE DOLPHINS FLY AND TURTLES PLAY
HERE YOU CAN LIVE YOUR LIFE AS A SEXY GIRL
LAHAMI BAY

LET IT FLOW
(BUTTERFLY)

LET IT FLOW, LET IT FLOW
HERE WE GO, MY DARLING
LET IT GROW, LET IT GROW
LET IT FLOW, SWEET LADY

YOU AND I, YOU AND I
TOUCH THE SKY SO EASY
ME AND YOU, ME AND YOU
RENDEZVOUS SO LONELY

NOW IN THE MIDDLE OF THE NIGHT
LOVE, IT'S THE FIRST TIME WE UNITE
JUST FEEL YOUR BODY FLYIN' HIGH
THEN KISS ME GENTLY, BUTTERFLY

GIVE ME LOVE, ALL YOUR LOVE
SHOW ME LIGHTS OF HEAVEN
I CAN FEEL, YES, I FEEL
YOU'VE BEEN THERE BEFORE THEN

IN MY MIND, IN MY MIND
YOU'RE A CUTE SWEET VIRGIN
BUT I KNOW, YES, I KNOW
TALENT SHOWS THE TRUTH, MAN

NOW IN THE MIDDLE OF THE NIGHT
LOVE, IT'S THE FIRST TIME WE UNITE
JUST FEEL YOUR BODY FLYIN' HIGH
THEN KISS ME GENTLY, BUTTERFLY

LIEBE MEINES LEBENS

DER REGEN FÄLLT AUF MEINEN KOPF STUNDENLANG
ICH STARRE ALLEIN VOR MICH HIN AUF DER BANK

ICH KANN ES NICHT VERSTEHEN
ICH KANN ES NICHT MEHR SPÜREN
DIE LIEBE MEINES LEBENS
LIESS MICH EINFACH GEHEN

WARUM IST DIE WELT WIE SIE WAR?
ICH SCHREIE DOCH DANN WIRD MIR KLAR:
DU BIST HIER!
ICH KÖNNTE DOCH EINFACH VERSTEHEN
ICH KÖNNTE DOCH EINFACH DEN WEG ZU DIR GEHEN
EIN SMALLTALK JUST FOR TWO
EIN KLEINES RENDEZVOUS
MÖCHTEST DU MICH SEHEN
UND WIEDER HAND IN HAND
MIT MIR DURCH UNSER LEBEN GEHEN?

VIELLEICHT WAR ICH MUTIG UND KLUG ALS ICH GING
VIELLEICHT WAR ICH BOCKIG UND STUR, OHNE SINN

ICH KANN ES NICHT MEHR ÄNDERN
ICH KANN ES NICHT VERSTEHEN
DIE LIEBE MEINES LEBENS
LIESS MICH EINFACH GEHEN

WARUM IST DIE WELT WIE SIE WAR?
ICH SCHREIE DOCH DANN WIRD MIR KLAR:
DU BIST HIER!
ICH KÖNNTE DOCH EINFACH VERSTEHEN
ICH KÖNNTE DOCH EINFACH DEN WEG ZU DIR GEHEN
EIN SMALLTALK JUST FOR TWO
EIN KLEINES RENDEZVOUS
MÖCHTEST DU MICH SEHEN
UND WIEDER HAND IN HAND
MIT MIR DURCH UNSER LEBEN GEHEN?

LIFE IS A TEST FOR THE BEST

SUNDAY LONELY
CAN´T SLEEP NO MORE
TURNING TO BEDSIDE
I HEAR A KNOCK ON THE DOOR

PETER POSTMAN
IT´S HIM AGAIN
DAY OFF, HE´S LONELY
HE LOOKS AT ME AS A FRIEND

TALKING SO MUCH
DRINKING BEER AND ONE MORE WINE
UGLY THE TEARS
AND THE FEARS WE LEAVE BEHIND
PETER, MY FRIEND
I UNDERSTAND
LIFE IS A TEST FOR THE BEST

PETER POSTMAN
LEFT BY HIS WIFE
LOST HIS 2 CHILDREN
HIS HOUSE AND NEARLY HIS LIFE

SAME OLD STORY
MY LIFE IS DONE
LOST MY WHOLE FAMILY
MY WIFE, MY DAUGHTER, MY SON

TALKING SO MUCH
DRINKING BEER AND ONE MORE WINE
UGLY THE TEARS
AND THE FEARS WE LEAVE BEHIND
PETER, MY FRIEND
I UNDERSTAND
LIFE IS A TEST FOR THE BEST

LIFE OF A CLOWN

SUN'S GOING DOWN
LIFE OF A CLOWN
SMILING FOR YOU
YOU LOVE ME TOO

SHOW STARTS AGAIN
THIS TIME, MY FRIEND
LAST NIGHT FOR ME
THEN I'LL BE FREE

ALL OF MY LIFE I'M IN THE LIGHTS
TAKE ME AWAY AS DARKNESS BITES
FOR THE END
ALL OF MY LIFE I WAS THE CLOWN
PUTTING YOU UP AND MYSELF DOWN
GOING DOWN

SO MANY YEARS
TOO MANY BEERS
PUSHING MYSELF
NOW I NEED HELP

ALL OF MY LIFE I'M IN THE LIGHTS
TAKE ME AWAY AS DARKNESS BITES
FOR THE END
ALL OF MY LIFE I WAS THE CLOWN
PUTTING YOU UP AND MYSELF DOWN
GOING DOWN

LIVE AND EXIST OR LIVE AND ENJOY

AN ORANGE BED IN THE LIVING ROOM
A DUSTY CHAIR JUST FOR TWO
NO PLACE TO COOK FOR GERONIMO
BUT HERE WE LIVE, ME AND YOU

HOW CAN WE MAKE A BETTER LIFE?
CAN WE AFFORD SOME BETTER TIMES?
IT AIN´T RIGHT

CAN WE LIVE AND EXIST
OR LIVE AND ENJOY WHAT WE´VE MISSED
IN A LAND FAR AWAY?
WHERE THE MONDAYS ARE GREEN
AND WHITE, DO YOU KNOW WHAT I MEAN?
IN A LAND FAR AWAY

A GREEN BALLOON, I HAVE SEEN THE LIGHT
A KISS OF LOVE JUST FOR YOU
AND COMES THE NIGHT WE WILL FLY AWAY
INTO THE LAND WE WILL STAY

WE TAKE A CHANCE OF SOMETHING NEW
UP AND AWAY INTO THE BLUE
ME AND YOU

WE CAN LIVE AND EXIST
WE LIVE AND ENJOY WHAT WE´VE MISSED
IN A LAND FAR AWAY
WHERE THE SUNDAYS ARE GREEN
AND WHITE, DO YOU KNOW WHAT I MEAN?
IN A LAND FAR AWAY

LEAVING THE DUSTY CHAIR BEHIND
FEELING SO FREE NOW IN MY MIND
IT´S ALL RIGHT

LIVE OR DIE

DRIVING FAST FAR TOO STRONG
AS I KEEP ON MOVING ON
SUDDENLY CAR THAT TURNS
AND A CRASH, MY BODY BURNS
LOSING ALL MY FRIENDS
IN A WHIRL

VISION OF ME LIVE OR DIE
CHANGING ROUND ABOUT
FATHER ABOVE I BELIEVE IN MY LIFE
BROKEN MY BONES
CAN THEY HEAL?
IS IT WORTHLESS NOW?
STRONGER I FEEL NOW FOR SURE
LIVE OR DIE

I WS FAST, I WAS STRONG
I WAS RIDING ALL ALONG
ON MY WAY TO MY GIRL
I WAS HAPPY IN MY WORLD
BOUGHT HER PRETTY PEARLS
GOLD AND WHITE

VISION OF ME LIVE OR DIE
CHANGING ROUND ABOUT
FATHER ABOVE I BELIEVE IN MY LIFE
BROKEN MY BONES
CAN THEY HEAL?
IS IT WORTHLESS NOW?
STRONGER I FEEL NOW FOR SURE
LIVE OR DIE

I FEEL NEW PAIN
ONE MORE AGAIN
ONE MORE I FEEL
HARD AND REAL

LOOKING FOR ANOTHER LOVE

NEED TO COME ANOTHER DAY
I'M OUT OF TIME
CAUSE SOMEONE IS INNOCENT
NEED TO FIND ANOTHER WAY
TO TALK WITH YOU
ABOUT OUR RELATIONSHIP

AS I TURN AND WALK AWAY
I SEE YOUR FACE GETS READY TO SMILE
I WILL COME ANOTHER DAY
YOU'RE GETTIN' HIGH

I DON'T NEVER GIVE A DAMN
AS I SEE YOUR BELAVISTA MAN
IF YOU'RE READY TO DECIDE
JUST LEAVE THE MAN
I WAS ALL DAY AND NIGHT

NEED MY MONEY NOT FOR YOU
WHY SHOULD I PAY YOU
THOUSANDS OF BUCKS I HAVE?
NEED TO FIND OUT IF IT'S TRUE
THE WORD I HEARD
YOU STOLE MY MAJESTIC CAR

SHALL I FIND ANOTHER LOVE?
SO MANY GIRLS INTERESTED IN ME
LOOKING FOR ANOTHER LOVE
WHO WILL IT BE?

I DON'T NEVER GIVE A DAMN
AS I SEE YOUR BELAVISTA MAN
IF YOU'RE READY TO DECIDE
JUST LEAVE THE MAN
I WAS ALL DAY AND NIGHT

LOOKING FOR MY BABY

LOOKING FOR MY BABY
AND I´M LOOKING FOR THE DAY
BABY COMES ALONG THIS ROAD
AND BABY COMES MY WAY
SINCE SHE LEFT ME I´M ALONE
SHE´S NEVER COMING BACK
SHE WAS ALL I HAD AND MORE
THE BEST I EVER HAD
EVEN WHEN THE WORLD GOES DOWN
I WON´T FORGET HER SMILE
EVEN WHEN I SEE HER KISS
ANOTHER HANDSOME GUY
LOOKING FOR MY BABY
AND I´M DREAMING OF ANOTHER CHANCE AGAIN
MISSING YOU FOREVER
I´M IN LOVE WITH YOU UNTIL THE DAYS WILL END

WAKE UP EARLY MORNING
AND I LAY DOWN LATE AT NIGHT
LOOKING FOR MY BABY
TIL THE LAST OF ME HAS DIED
DREAMING OF THE PARADISE
YOU SHOWED ME EVERY DAY
WE HAD TALKS TO MARRY
ON THE 17TH OF MAY
OUT OF NOWHERE, OUT OF SIGHT
YOU LEFT ME IN THE GREY
DIDN´T KNOW THE REASON THOUGH
UNTIL THIS VERY DAY
LOOKING FOR MY BABY
SHE´S THE ONLY ONE ESTABLISHED BY MY SIDE
WILL I FIND THE TRUTH OF THIS
AND WILL SHE SOMEHOW BE MY PRETTY BRIDE?

IF YOUR HEART IS FEELING NOW THE SAME
BE ADVISED I´LL TAKE YOU BACK AGAIN
IF YOU THINK OF ALL THE FUNNY DAYS
WE CAN STOP AND FINISH NOW THE CHASE
ONLY LONELY IS MY HEART OF GOLD
TAKE ME BACK BEFORE I´M GETTING OLD
YOU I KNOW ARE HIDING IN THE DARK
CAN YOU FEEL MY LONESOME PRETTY HEART?

LOOKING FOR MY BABY
AND I´M LOOKING FOR THE DAY
BABY COMES ALONG THIS ROAD
AND BABY COMES MY WAY
SINCE SHE LEFT ME I´M ALONE
SHE´S NEVER COMING BACK
SHE WAS ALL I HAD AND MORE
THE BEST I EVER HAD
EVEN WHEN THE WORLD GOES DOWN
I WON´T FORGET HER SMILE
EVEN WHEN I SEE HER KISS
ANOTHER HANDSOME GUY
LOOKING FOR MY BABY
AND I´M DREAMING OF ANOTHER CHANCE AGAIN
MISSING YOU FOREVER
I´M IN LOVE WITH YOU UNTIL THE DAYS WILL END

WAKE UP EARLY MORNING
AND I LAY DOWN LATE AT NIGHT
LOOKING FOR MY BABY
TIL THE LAST OF ME HAS DIED
DREAMING OF THE PARADISE
YOU SHOWED ME EVERY DAY
WE HAD TALKS TO MARRY
ON THE 17TH OF MAY
OUT OF NOWHERE, OUT OF SIGHT
YOU LEFT ME IN THE GREY
DIDN´T KNOW THE REASON THOUGH
UNTIL THIS VERY DAY
LOOKING FOR MY BABY
SHE´S THE ONLY ONE ESTABLISHED BY MY SIDE
WILL I FIND THE TRUTH OF THIS
AND WILL SHE SOMEHOW BE MY PRETTY BRIDE?

IF YOUR HEART IS FEELING NOW THE SAME
BE ADVISED I´LL TAKE YOU BACK AGAIN
IF YOU THINK OF ALL THE FUNNY DAYS
WE CAN STOP AND FINISH NOW THE CHASE
ONLY LONELY IS MY HEART OF GOLD
TAKE ME BACK BEFORE I´M GETTING OLD
YOU I KNOW ARE HIDING IN THE DARK
CAN YOU FEEL MY LONESOME PRETTY HEART?

LOSING MY HEART TO THIS GIRL

I MET A GIRL
I FELL IN LOVE
I GAVE HER ALL MY SWEETEST LOVE
AS YOU CAN HEAR
THE STORY´S SAD
SHE KICKED ME STRAIGHT OUT OF HER BED

ON THE STREETS
ON THE RUN

THINKING OF HER EVERY DAY AND EVERY NIGHT
SHE IS THE ONE I WILL MISS THROUGH ALL MY LIFE
NEVER AGAIN WILL I FIND SUCH A LOVE
TEARS IN MY EYES NEVER DRY NOT ENOUGH
LOSING MY HEART TO THIS GIRL
I´D GIVE HER ALL IN THE WORLD
MARY-ANN

WE HAD ONE NIGHT
WE HAD ONE SLEEP
WE HAD ONE KISS, WE HAD ONE CHEAT
ALL OF YOUR WORDS
ALL OF YOUR SMILE
ALL OF YOUR MOUTH, YOU SAID GOODBYE

KICKED ME OUT
THROUGH THE DOOR

THINKING OF YOU EVERY DAY AND EVERY NIGHT
YOU ARE THE ONE I WILL MISS THROUGH ALL MY LIFE
NEVER AGAIN WILL I FIND SUCH A LOVE
TEARS IN MY EYES NEVER DRY NOT ENOUGH
LOSING MY HEART TO YOU, GIRL
I´D GIVE YOU ALL IN THE WORLD
MARY-ANN

LOST A LIFE OF SUNSHINE

SOME 20 YEARS OF YOU AND I
WE SHARED OUR LOVE UNTIL WE CRIED
IT WASN'T EASY AS THEY SAY
BUT NOW'S THE TIME TO RUN AWAY

IT WAS THEATER HOW IT CAME THAT WAY
BUT I DECIDED CALLING IT A DAY
YOU LOOKED AT GEORGIE AND IT BROKE MY HEART
AND THAT'S WHY WE FELL APART

WE LOST A LIFE OF SUNSHINE
OUR LIVING WASN'T BAD
YOU HAD YOUR SHARE OF BOY TOYS
BUT GEORGIE DROVE ME MAD
CAUSE HE'S MY LITTLE BABY
MY BROTHER AS YOU KNOW
YOU KICKED MY UNDERSTANDING
AND WHILE YOU FUCKED HIM
I PREFER TO GO

SOME 20 YEARS OF YOU AND I
WE SHARED SOME LOVE I CAN'T DENY
YOU WERE THE SPECIAL ONE FOR SURE
BUT I CAN'T TAKE IT ANYMORE

IT WAS THEATER ON THE DAY OF PAIN
I SAW YOU LAUGHING AND IT WAS A SHAME
MY LITTLE BROTHER LOOKED INTO YOUR EYES
I COULDN'T BEAT THAT SURPRISE

WE LOST A LIFE OF SUNSHINE
OUR LIVING WASN'T BAD
YOU HAD YOUR SHARE OF BOY TOYS
BUT GEORGIE DROVE ME MAD
CAUSE HE'S MY LITTLE BABY
MY BROTHER AS YOU KNOW
YOU KICKED MY UNDERSTANDING
AND WHILE YOU FUCKED HIM
I PREFER TO GO

LOVE IS LIKE A MIRACLE

LOVE IS LIKE A MIRACLE IN THE WIND
I LOVE AND LIVE A SPECIAL ONE NOT A THING

EVERY NIGHT I RUN AWAY
FAR AWAY INTO THE NIGHT
TO A PLACE WHERE MAGIC DREAMS
COME ALIVE

LOVE IS LIKE A MIRACLE
I TRY TO CATCH THE LIGHT
NEARLY IT´S FANATICAL
NOW FANTASY´S ALIVE
HOLD ME UP TONIGHT
DREAMS AND DREAMS
AND MORE SWEET DREAMS IN THE NIGHT

JOY IS LIKE A MIRACLE OF THE SKY
A SKY SO BLUE AND FAR AWAY FROM MY TIME

NOW IT´S TIME TO TURN AROUND
AS THE SKY BEGINS TO SHINE
TO A PLACE WHERE MAGICAL
WILL BE MINE

LOVE IS LIKE A MIRACLE
I TRY TO CATCH THE LIGHT
NEARLY IT´S FANATICAL
NOW FANTASY´S ALIVE
HOLD ME UP TONIGHT
DREAMS AND DREAMS
AND MORE SWEET DREAMS IN THE NIGHT

WILL YOU ASK ME WHY I GO?
WILL YOU TRY TO HOLD MY HAND?
WILL YOU WAVE GOODBYE
AS I FLY TO MY LAND?

LOVING LINES

I SAW YOU STANDING IN THE PARK
AS SUN AND TIME GOT SLOWLY DARK
I TOOK A WALK ON DOWN TO YOU
AND ASKED YOU WHERE YOU´RE GOING TO

YOU DIDN´T ANSWER WITH YOUR EYES
A KISS OF MAGIC, BIG SURPRISE

TAKE ME NOW TO THE LOVING LINES
TAKE ME UP TO YOUR PARADISE
ON THE ROAD TO THE MAGIC HOUSE
MAGIC TIMES WE CONSIDER IN THIS HOUSE
I LOVE YOU, SAYS YOUR MOUTH

AFTER A NIGHT OF JOY AND FUN
CONSIDERING THAT WE ARE DONE
YOU OPEN UP YOUR PRETTY EYES
IT´S MORE YOU OPEN, BIG SURPRISE

FORGET THIS KIND OF ONE NIGHT STAND
LET´S STAY TOGETHER TIL THE END

TAKE ME NOW TO THE LOVING LINES
TAKE ME UP TO YOUR PARADISE
ON THE ROAD TO THE MAGIC HOUSE
MAGIC TIMES WE CONSIDER IN THIS HOUSE
I LOVE YOU, SAYS YOUR MOUTH

M - O

MAN IN BLACK

TAKE THE NIGHT AWAY
SKY IS DULL AND GREY
BLOOD INSIDE MY BED
SWORD BENEATH MY HEAD

WHAT A DREAM I HAD TO DREAM!
MAN IN BLACK WAS PRETTY MEAN

CLOSE MY EYES AND AWAY
DARKNESS FALLS BUT I´M OK
IT´S A DREAM I JUST DREAM
HERE WITH ME
MAN IN BLACK COMES AGAIN
TAKES ME FORTH AND BACK AGAIN
SCARY EYES TAKE A RIDE
MYSTERY

PAIN, I KNOW THIS GAME
FAME, IT´S ALL FOR FAME
DOWN, DEEP DOWN I CRY
CLOSE, I NEARLY DIE

IT´S A DREAM AND SO UNREAL
THOUGH THE PAIN I REALLY FEEL

CLOSE YOUR EYES AND AWAY
DARKNESS FALLS BUT YOU´RE OK
IT´S A DREAM YOU JUST DREAM
HERE WITH ME
MAN IN BLACK COMES AGAIN
TAKES YOU FORTH AND BACK AGAIN
SCARY EYES TAKE A RIDE
MYSTERY

MAN OF GOLD
(SAVING LITTLE YOU)

A MAN OF GOLD IN HIS BEST YEARS
SHAKING HIS COIN AND DRINKING BEERS
NEVER UNDERSTOOD, NEVER UNDERSTAND
YOU AS A COMMON MAN
LIVING MY LIFE SAILING THE SEAS
CRUISIN´ AWAY INTO THE BREEZE
WHERE IS NOW? WATCHING THE SUN
SHINING TOWARDS THIS BOAT I COME
IS IT REALLY TRUE? PARADISE IS HERE
I SEE A GIRL IN FEAR
THIS IS MY TIME, THIS IS MY PLACE
TAKE HER ON BOARD AND LEAVE THIS PLACE

HEY NOW, WHERE ARE WE GOING TO?
WE CRUISE ANOTHER DAY UNTIL THE SKY IS GREY
HEY NOW, I´M SAVING LITTLE YOU, THE MAN OF GOLD

I SAW YOU THERE NAKED AND WEAK
LOST ON THE SEA AND SO IN NEED
DIDN´T TAKE A LOOK, DIDN´T SAY A WORD
GAVE YOU MY PLAYBOY SHIRT
SOMETHING TO EAT, SOMETHING TO DRINK
GENTLEMAN´S BED BUT NOT IN PINK
YOU WAKE UP NOW WITH A SMILE
SEEING IN FRONT OF YOU THIS ISLE
THIS IS WHERE I LIVE, THIS IS WHAT I AM
I´M CALLED A SELF-MADE-MAN
NOW IT IS TIME THANK YOU TO SAY
AND I JUST KNOW THE PERFECT WAY

HEY NOW, WHERE ARE WE GOING TO?
WE KISS ANOTHER DAY UNTIL THE SKY IS GREY
HEY NOW, I´M SO IN LOVE WITH YOU, SEE-BROKEN GIRL

I FEEL YOUR LOVE HEALTHY AND STRONG
7 DAYS LATER LEAVING HOME
CRUISIN´ ALL AROUND ALL THE 7 SEAS
YOU THERE UPON YOUR KNEES
BLOWING THE WIND, BLOWING MY MIND
YOU ARE THE ONE I HAD TO FIND

MANN IM MOND

DA WO ALL DIE STERNE SIND
DA BIN ICH ZUHAUS
SCHAU HINAB UND SCHALT DAS LICHTLEIN AUS
UNTER MIR DIE WELT SO KLEIN
ICH BIN SO WEIT WEG
DENN ICH BIN DER MANN IM MOND
LIEG IN MEINEM BETT

UND SCHON WIEDER EIN KIND GEBOREN
WIEDER EIN LICHT DAS GEHT
UND DER MANN IM MOND TRÄUMT VON DAMALS
BLICKT ZURÜCK AUF DEN WEG
HOCH IN SEIN HAUS
IN SEINEM HAUS

JEDEN TAG IM SONNENSCHEIN
JEDE NACHT IM MOND
HIER BIN ICH, DER MOND IST JETZT BEWOHNT
DA WO ALL DIE STERNE SIND
BIN ICH JETZT ZUHAUS
DENN ICH BIN DER MANN IM MOND
SCHALT DIE LICHTER AUS

UND SCHON WIEDER EIN TAG VOLLENDET
WIEDER EIN TRAUM DER GEHT
MEINE SEHNSUCHT IST UNENDLICH
TRÄUME VON MEINEM WEG
HOCH IN MEIN HAUS
HOCH IN MEIN HAUS
BLICK INS WELTALL HINAUS

MEIN LIEBSTER FLUCH
(ONLINEWELT)

STUNDENLANG AUF FACEBOOK
WER HAT WELCHE NEWS?
GIBT ES ETWAS DAS ICH WISSEN MUSS?

WER HAT WELCHE FREUNDIN?
UND WIE SIEHT SIE AUS?
FRÜHER GING ICH WIRKLICH GERNE AUS
HEUTE KOMM ICH NUR NOCH SELTEN RAUS

ONLINEWELT
MEIN LIEBSTER FLUCH
ATEMLOS SURF ICH DURCH DIE NACHT
WEIL ICH MUSS
AUF DER SPUR
VOM ZEITGESCHEHEN
DIESE WELT HÄLT MICH FEST
SAG: WANN LÄSST SIE MICH GEHEN?

ONLINE-PARTNERSUCHE
SHOPPING-PARADIES
EINGESPERRT IN MEINEM TRAUMVERLIES

VIRTUELLES LEBEN
IST DER WEG ZUM GLÜCK
EINMAL UM DEN GLOBUS UND ZURÜCK
ICH VERLIER MEIN LEBEN STÜCK FÜR STÜCK

ONLINEWELT
MEIN LIEBSTER FLUCH
ATEMLOS SURF ICH DURCH DIE NACHT
WEIL ICH MUSS
AUF DER SPUR
VOM ZEITGESCHEHEN
DIESE WELT HÄLT MICH FEST
SAG: WANN LÄSST SIE MICH GEHEN?

MOLLY AND HOLLY BLUE
(10 AFTER 10)

10 AFTER 10
ON A STREET I AM WITH A FRIEND
THROUGH RAIN AND SNOW
ON OUR WAY TO „(*KUSS*)", HERE WE GO

SINCE WE ARE 21
SUNDAY´S THE DAY OF BIG FUN
MOLLY AND HOLLY BLUE
WE´RE WITH YOU

10 AFTER 10 TONIGHT
2 HANDSOME MEN, ALRIGHT
WE´RE ON OUR WAY TO YOU
OPEN YOUR EYES
MOLLY AND HOLLY BLUE
DEEP NOW INSIDE OF YOU
IT FEELS A BETTER WORLD
THAN HOLLYWOOD LIES

HOLLYWOOD LIES
EVERY DAY AND WAY SUPERSIZE
HOLLYWOOD DREAMS
FULL OF FUN WITH CUTE BEAUTY QUEENS

10 AFTER 10 AGAIN
HOLLYWOOD DREAMS COME AGAIN
MOLLY AND HOLLY BLUE
WE´RE WITH YOU

MAKE US SOME HAPPY MEN
10 OUT OF 10, MY FRIEND
THROUGH RAIN AND SNOW WE GO
UNTIL WE DIE
MOLLY AND HOLLY BLUE
FAVOURITE GIRLS ARE YOU
10 OUT OF 10 AGAIN
LOSING MY TIME

MÖCHTEST DU HEUT NACHT?
(VERSION 1)

ICH TANZE DICH AN DENN DU GEHÖRST ZU MIR
DIESE NACHT DER SEHNSUCHT
FÜHRT MICH NÄHER RAN ZU DIR
EIN BLICK WIE EIN KUSS, ICH BIN EUPHORISIERT
KOMM NOCH ETWAS NÄHER
ICH BIN HEUT MOTORISIERT
UND ZEIG DIR DIE WELT

MÖCHTEST DU HEUT NACHT ENDLOS MIT MIR TANZEN?
UND ICH SCHENKE DIR MEINE KLEINE WELT
MÖCHTEST DU HEUT NACHT
IN MEINEN ARMEN TRÄUMEN?
BIS DER TAG ERWACHT, ICH GEB DICH NICHT MEHR HER

EIN DRINK WIE EIN KUSS, ICH BIN HYPNOTISIERT
DEINE GROSSEN AUGEN
ICH BIN SPRACHLOS FASZINIERT
DAS LUSTDIAGRAMM STEIGT ENDLOS HOCH EMPOR
WORAUF SOLL ICH WARTEN?
DENN DER BALL MUSS JETZT INS TOR
ICH FLÜSTER DIR INS OHR:

MÖCHTEST DU HEUT NACHT ALL DIE STERNE SEHEN?
ICH ZEIG DIR DEN ORT WO DIE LIEBE WOHNT
MÖCHTEST DU HEUT NACHT EINIGES ERLEBEN
DASS DU NIE VERGISST WENN DU EWIG LEBST?

UH UH UH UH UH UH UH UH - UH UH UH UH UH UH UH

MÖCHTEST DU HEUT NACHT DICH MIT MIR VERGNÜGEN?
DENN ICH SCHENKE DIR MEINE KLEINE WELT
MÖCHTEST DU HEUT NACHT ALL DIE LIEBE SPÜREN
DIE IN MIR ERWACHT WENN DU BEI MIR BIST
MÖCHTEST DU HEUT NACHT?

MÖCHTEST DU HEUT NACHT?
(VERSION 2)

WIR TANZEN SOLANG DIE WELT SICH UM UNS DREHT
SEHNSUCHT UND DIE LIEBE
WIE EIN WINDRAUSCH UM UNS WEHT
EIN BLICK WIE EIN KUSS, TOTAL EUPHORISIERT
KOMM NOCH ETWAS NÄHER
ICH BIN SO FASZINIERT
HEUT ZEIG ICH DIR MEINE WELT

MÖCHTEST DU HEUT NACHT ENDLOS MIT MIR TANZEN?
UND ICH SCHENKE DIR EINE NEUE WELT
MÖCHTEST DU HEUT NACHT
IN MEINEN ARMEN TRÄUMEN?
BIS DER TAG ERWACHT, ICH GEB DICH NICHT MEHR HER

EIN ERSTER KUSS, ICH BIN HYPNOTISIERT
DEINE GROSSEN AUGEN
SPRACHLOS FASZINIERT
EIN LUSTDIAGRAMM STEIGT ENDLOS HOCH EMPOR
WORAUF SOLL ICH WARTEN?
WEISST DU, ICH HAB WAS VOR
UND ICH FLÜSTER DIR INS OHR:

MÖCHTEST DU HEUT NACHT ALL DIE STERNE SEHEN?
ICH ZEIG DIR DEN ORT WO DIE LIEBE WOHNT
MÖCHTEST DU HEUT NACHT EINIGES ERLEBEN
DASS DU NIE VERGISST WENN DU EWIG LEBST

UND IN DER NACHT
HAND IN HAND, BEGLEITET UNS DER MOND
AM STERNENZELT, EIN BLICK HINAUF
DORT WO DIE LIEBE WOHNT
ICH STREICHE DIR GANZ SANFT DURCHS HAAR
DU BIST NICHT MEHR ALLEIN
LASS UNS FÜR JETZT UND ALLE ZEIT
DAS UNIVERSUM SEIN

MVP IS BACK ALL RIGHT

I BELIEVE IN A MIRACLE
IN A FANTASY WHICH IS LOGICAL
CAN YOU FEEL THE HEAT OF THE DARKEST NIGHT?
CAN YOU MOVE AWAY TO THE STRONGEST LIGHT
IN MY DREAM?

YOU´RE THE ONE OUT OF PARADISE
PRETTY LEGS I SEE, SOME TERRIFIC EYES
WALKING DOWN THE ISLE IN THE CITY LIGHTS
SCENES OF PARADISE AND ROMANTIC NIGHTS
FULL OF JOY

MVP GOES CRAZY, HE BELIEVES HE´S IN A DREAM
FLASHING OFF HIS SHOULDERS
JUST FOR YOU HE´S VERY KEEN
OUT OF THE DARK, NEVER PLAYING WITH YOUR HEART
OUT OF THE NIGHT
MVP IS BACK ALL RIGHT

I BELIEVE IN A MIRACLE
IN A FANTASY WHICH IS LOGICAL
CAN YOU FEEL THE HEAT OF THE DARKEST NIGHT?
CAN YOU MOVE AWAY TO THE STRONGEST LIGHT
IN MY DREAM?

YOU´RE THE ONE OUT OF PARADISE
PRETTY LEGS I SEE, SOME TERRIFIC EYES
WALKING DOWN THE ISLE IN THE CITY LIGHTS
SCENES OF PARADISE AND ROMANTIC NIGHTS
FULL OF JOY

MVP GOES CRAZY, HE BELIEVES HE´S IN A DREAM
FLASHING OFF HIS SHOULDERS
JUST FOR YOU HE´S VERY KEEN
OUT OF THE DARK, NEVER PLAYING WITH YOUR HEART
OUT OF THE NIGHT
MVP IS BACK ALL RIGHT

MY LITTLE VIRGIN

SO MANY GIRLS AROUND
SCREAMING LIKE A CHILD
I´VE GOT A SEXY CROWD
DANCING, GOIN´ WILD

PLAYING SOME HOURS AWAY
JUST FOR THIS REDHEAD I SAY:

CLOSE YOUR BIG BROWN EYES
MY LITTLE VIRGIN
AND FEEL MY HANDS
UNDER YOUR SHIRT
FEEL THE BIG SURPRISE
MY LITTLE VIRGIN
I GOT FOR YOU
MY PRETTY BIRD

I´M RIGHT ON STAGE AGAIN
HANDSOME LIKE I AM
SO MANY GIRLS I SEE
SCREAMING, THEY WANT ME

I HEAR THIS BLONDE ONE TONIGHT
SHE IS THE RIGHT ONE, THAT´S RIGHT

CLOSE YOUR BIG BROWN EYES
MY LITTLE VIRGIN
AND FEEL MY HANDS
UNDER YOUR SHIRT
FEEL THE BIG SURPRISE
MY LITTLE VIRGIN
I GOT FOR YOU
MY PRETTY BIRD

MYSTERY SKY

SWORD IN MY HEAD
I´M BLEEDING TO DIE
NEXT LIFE WILL COME
AWAY NOW I FLY

MYSTERY SKY
A MYSTERY TRAIN
WHERE AM I NOW?
A NEW LIFE AGAIN

UH UH UH UH UH UH UH
UH UH UH UH UH UH UH

AGAIN I FLY INTO THE SKY
AGAIN I CRY, I HAVE TO DIE
ANOTHER LIFE NOW HERE I START
ANOTHER DEATH BREAKS ME APART

STOMACH IS WARM
I´M CUDDLING INSIDE
HAVE TO GET OUT
AT 12 IN THE NIGHT

FATHER IS TALL
HE´S LOOKING AT ME
I´M NOW A GIRL
A MAN I SHOULD BE

UH UH UH UH UH UH UH
UH UH UH UH UH UH UH

AGAIN I FLY INTO THE SKY
AGAIN I CRY, I HAVE TO DIE
ANOTHER LIFE NOW HERE I START
ANOTHER DEATH BREAKS ME APART

NAKED AGAIN

I SEE YOU NAKED AGAIN
LONG AGO YOU WERE BY MY SIDE
SO MANY YEARS NOW HAVE GONE
STILL I LIKE WHAT I SEE
PERFECT BODY JUST FOR ME

WHEN OUR BODIES UNITE
WHEN WE COME
I REMEMBER THE DAYS
OF GOOD FUN
YOU AND I
ARE YOU READY FOR ONE MORE TRY?

I KISS YOU DOWNSTAIRS AGAIN
STILL I LIKE THE SWEET TASTE OF YOU
I CAN´T REMEMBER THE TIME
WE WERE CLOSE, WE WERE SURE
IT CAME DIFFERENT, I HAD MORE

WE CAN DO IT AGAIN
STILL IT´S LOVE
OUR BODIES UNITE
FALL IN LOVE
YOU AND I
GIVE IT UP FOR ANOTHER TRY
WITHOUT WINGS WE CAN FLY

NO FEAR!

FAST AS DOGS
RUNNING AWAY FROM SOMETHING THEY DON´T KNOW
LIKE A FOX, FOX ON THE RUN
THEY FEEL THE MIGHTY BLOW
JUNE 25 WILL MARK ANOTHER LOW
FAR AWAY TO GO

NO FEAR! NOTHING TO SCARE
DEMONS SO FAR AWAY
SO NEAR VOICES OF LOVE
CALLING MY NAME
NO FEAR! NO NEED TO HIDE
NO NEED TO RUN AWAY
I AM HERE TO STAY

ANGRY BIRDS
FLAPPING THEIR WINGS AND TRY TO FLY AWAY
SCARY WORDS UP IN MY MIND
THEY TELL ME NOT TO STAY
FLYING AROUND INSIDE MY LITTLE BRAIN
CALLING NOW MY NAME

NO FEAR! NOTHING TO SCARE
DEMONS SO FAR AWAY
SO NEAR VOICES OF LOVE
CALLING MY NAME
NO FEAR! NO NEED TO HIDE
NO NEED TO RUN AWAY
I AM HERE TO STAY

LOSING LOVE
WHATEVER HAPPENED TO MY PRETTY LIFE
HIGH ABOVE POWERS THAT BE
PROMOTING HARDCORE NIGHTS
WHATEVER HAPPENED TO THE CITY LIGHTS
AND THE CITY RIGHTS

NOCH EIN LETZTER TANGO

VERGANGEN SIND DIE TAGE NUR MIT DIR
VERSCHLOSSEN UNSERE HERZEN UND DIE TÜR
DIE UNS DIE LIEBE SCHENKTE
DIE UNS DIE LIEBE NAHM
VERBUNDEN ALLE WUNDEN
DIE ICH SPÜREN KANN

NOCH EIN LETZTER TANGO
GANZ OHNE EMOTION
DIESEN EINEN TANGO
LAUF MIR NICHT DAVON
UNSERE BESTEN TAGE
LIEGEN IM DUNKLEN SCHON
NOCH EIN LETZTER TANGO
GANZ OHNE EMOTION

VERDROSSEN IST DIE LIEBE ZWISCHEN UNS
VERLOREN ALL DIE TRÄNEN KUGELRUND
ES WAR NICHTS MEHR ZU ÄNDERN
DAS LETZTE WORT GESAGT
DER ABSCHIED HEILT DIE WUNDEN
ES KOMMT EIN NEUER TAG

NOCH EIN LETZTER TANGO
GANZ OHNE EMOTION
DIESEN EINEN TANGO
LAUF MIR NICHT DAVON
UNSERE BESTEN TAGE
LIEGEN IM DUNKLEN SCHON
NOCH EIN LETZTER TANGO
GANZ OHNE EMOTION

NOW THE LEGEND IS DEAD
(RICKY PARFITT)

NOW THE LEGEND IS DEAD
I CAN´T BELIEVE
HE IS ROCKING TO GOD
CHRISTMAS EVE
68 YEARS OF FUN
HE ROCKED THE WORLD
WROTE QUITE HUNDREDS OF HITS
ALL YOU HAVE HEARD

RICKY PARFITT IS DEAD
GOODBYE, HERO
MR. RHYTHM MACHINE
LEFT THIS PLACE
NOW HE´S ROCKING WITH GOD
AND THE OTHERS
SOMEWHERE IN SPACE

NOW MY HERO IS GONE
I FEEL THE PAIN
HE MUST FELT IN HIS HEART
LIKE A FLAME
LIVED A LIFE ON THE ROAD
OF ROCK´N´ROLL
MANY PUSSYS ON BOARD
AND ALCOHOL

RICKY PARFITT IS DEAD
GOODBYE, HERO
MR. RHYTHM MACHINE
LEFT THIS PLACE
NOW HE´S ROCKING WITH GOD
AND THE OTHERS
SOMEWHERE IN SPACE

NUDE AND FREE

7 TO 8 IN THE NIGHT
SUDDENLY I SEE A LIGHT
LIGHT IS SO STRONG IN MY EYES
FEELING A MAGIC SURPRISE

AH AH AH AH - AH AH AH AH

YOU CAN´T BELIEVE WHAT I SEE
WOMEN AND MEN NUDE AND FREE
WHERE DO THEY COME FROM AND WHY?
PLAYING THEIR GAMES IN THE NIGHT

UH UH UH UH - UH UH UH UH

WOMEN AND MEN IN THE NIGHT
SEXY AND FREE THEY UNITE
SHOULD I BE PART OF THEIR GAME?
SHOULD I REVEAL THEM MY NAME?
NO, NO, CAN´T GO
CAN´T PLAY THIS GAME NOW WITH YOU
NO, NO, WINDOW
THROUGH I SEE ALL WHAT THEY DO

CRAZY IS NOW WHAT I SEE
WOMEN AND MEN NUDE AND FREE
HAVING GOOD SEX AND GOOD FUN
I KNOW SOME LIVES JUST BEGUN

AH AH AH AH - AH AH AH AH

WOMEN AND MEN IN THE NIGHT
SEXY AND FREE THEY UNITE
SHOULD I BE PART OF THEIR GAME?
SHOULD I REVEAL THEM MY NAME?
NO, NO, CAN´T GO
CAN´T PLAY THIS GAME NOW WITH YOU
NO, NO, WINDOW
THROUGH I SEE ALL WHAT THEY DO

OHNE DICH WILL ICH NICHT

GRAD ERWACHT UND DER TAG GEHT LOS
ICH BIN TRAURIG DENN ICH BIN ALLEIN
STEIG AUFS RAD, FAHR ZUM ARZT
FÜHL MICH KRANK OHNE DICH GANZ ALLEIN

GESTERN NACHT WAR DIE NACHT
VOLLER LIEBE UND ROSEN
DU DRÜCKTEST MICH FESTER AN DICH
TAUSEND KÜSSE UND HERZEN VERFÜHRTEN
DIE UNSCHULD DER STERNE
DIE UNSCHULD ZERBRACH

OHNE DICH WILL ICH NICHT
OHNE DICH BIN ICH NICHT

DÜSTERE WOLKEN UND TRAUER
GESPENSTISCHE SCHATTEN SIND ÜBERALL
DU BIST SO WEIT FORT
ICH GLAUB ICH SCHIESS MICH SELBST GLEICH INS ALL

TRAURIG IM BETT
WO BIST DU? WER BIN ICH?
DIESES WARTEN, EIN GRAUEN DER ZEIT
BIS DU KLOPFST HEUTE NACHT, DU UND ICH
ICH BIN JETZT SCHON BEREIT
MEINE LIEBE BEFREIT

OHNE DICH WILL ICH NICHT
JA, OHNE DICH BIN ICH NICHT
OHNE DICH WILL ICH NICHT, NEIN, NEIN, NEIN
OHNE NICHT BIN ICH NICHT, BIN ICH NICHT

KOMM JETZT NÄHER ZU MIR
UND BEGLÜCKE DICH MIT MIR
SCHENK MIR EINE NACHT
VOLLER LIEBE, HIEBE, TRIEBE
UND EINEN KUSS

OK!
(FRAU)

ICH STEHE NACKT VOR DIR
DU, DU STEHST NACKT VOR MIR
WIR HABEN SO VIEL VOR
KÜSS MICH, AMOR
ICH ZEIG DIR DAS GLÜCK
DU GIBST ES MIR ZURÜCK
WIR SIND EIN SONNENPAAR
WUNDERBAR

OK! DIE HÄNDE DIE SIND ÜBERALL
OK! DIE KÜSSE SCHARF WIE DONNERHALL
OK! ICH BIN DIE PRETTY DRAMA QUEEN
OK, OK, OK!
OK! DIE TYPEN WOLLEN MEIN AUTOGRAMM
OK! HEUT ABEND SUCH ICH MIR´N MANN
OK! DIE NACHT WIRD WILD, DAS WEISS ICH SCHON
OK, OK, OK!

DICH NEHME ICH HEUT NACHT
DU, DU HAST MICH ENTFACHT
ICH WILL DIE STERNE SEHEN
LEIDENSCHAFT
JA, ICH BIN DIR VERFALLEN
KOMM, LASS UNS NOCHMAL („*PFIFF*")
DU LIEGST IN MEINEM BETT
NUR HEUT NACHT

OK! LICHT AUS UND JETZT VERFÜHR ICH DICH
OK! DIE POST GEHT AB, DU STEICHELST MICH
OK! ICH BIN DIE PRETTY DRAMA QUEEN
OK, OK, OK!
OK! ICH SPÜR DIE LIEBE TIEF IN MIR
OK! MEIN HELD, UND JETZT BESORG ICH´S DIR
OK! DIE NACHT IST JUNG, WIR LIEBEN UNS
OK, OK, OK!
OK, OK, OK!

OK!
(MANN)

ICH STEHE NUN VOR DIR
DU, DU STEHST NUN VOR MIR
WIR HABEN SO VIEL VOR
DU LIEBST AMOR
ICH ZEIG DIR DAS GLÜCK
DU GIBST ES MIR ZURÜCK
WIR SIND EIN SONNENPAAR
WUNDERBAR

OK! DIE HÄNDE DIE SIND ÜBERALL
OK! DIE KÜSSE SCHARF WIE DONNERHALL
OK! ICH BIN DER GROSSE ZAMPANO
OK, OK, OK!
OK! DIE MÄDELS WOLLEN MEIN AUTOGRAMM
OK! DIE HÄNDE DIE SIND ÜBERALL
OK! ICH BIN DER MANN IM RADIO
OK, OK, OK!

DICH NEHME ICH HEUT NACHT
ICH HAB AN DICH GEDACHT
WIR WERDEN DIE STERNE SEHEN
UND NOCH VIEL MEHR
DU BIST MIR VERFALLEN
LUST-KÜSSE ÜBERALL
DU LIEGST IN MEINEM BETT
SCHAUST MICH AN

OK! LICHT AUS UND JETZT VERFÜHR ICH DICH
OK! DIE POST GEHT AB, DU STEICHELST MICH
OK! ICH BIN DER GROSSE ZAMPANO
OK, OK, OK!
OK! ICH SPÜR DIE LIEBE TIEF IN DIR
OK! ICH FÜHL DIE LIEBE AUCH IN MIR
OK! ICH BIN DER MANN IM RADIO
OK, OK, OK!
OK, OK, OK!

ONE NIGHT STAND

NOW PLEASE FORGIVE ME
I SWEAR SHE´S AWAY
YES, I BETRAYED YOU ONE DAY

SHE WAS DELICIOUS
HER EYES MADE ME WEAK
SHE TOOK CONTROL OF MY FEET

WE HAD A SIMPLE ONE NIGHT STAND
JUST ONE NIGHT ONLY, UNDERSTAND
SHE´S AWAY, LEFT INTO THE GREY
NOW PLEASE FORGIVE ME AND BELIEVE
I´LL NEVER EVER PACK AND LEAVE
HOLD ME TIGHT EVERY DAY AND NIGHT

TEARS, FEARS AND MADNESS
YOU SEEM QUITE IN RAGE
AND INTERESTED IN HER AGE

WELL, LET ME TELL YOU
OF COURSE SHE WAS YOUNG
IT WAS A NIGHT OF JUST FUN

WE HAD A SIMPLE ONE NIGHT STAND
JUST ONE NIGHT ONLY, UNDERSTAND
SHE´S AWAY, LEFT INTO THE GREY
NOW PLEASE FORGIVE ME AND BELIEVE
I´LL NEVER EVER PACK AND LEAVE
HOLD ME TIGHT EVERY DAY AND NIGHT

OUT OF THE DARK

MYSTERIES OF TIME
LOVE IN THE AIR
LOVE ALL AROUND EVERYWHERE
TAKING THE LIGHT
FROM ALL THE STARS
TAKING A CHOOSE OF ALL THE CARS
DRIVING AWAY

MAKING A BREAK
FREEDOM I FEEL
NOW WHERE I AM, IS IT REAL?
ANGELS I SEE
UP IN THE SKY
UP ON THE HILL I TRY TO FLY
FLYING AWAY

LEAVING THE EARTH AND FLYING AWAY
AS LONG AS I FLY I´M FEELING OK
LEAVING BEHIND MY BODY NOW
FLYING AWAY ALRIGHT SOMEHOW
LEAVING THIS PLACE
LEAVING THIS MESS
FOREVER NOW

MANKIND IS STRONG
PEOPLE ARE WEAK
PROBLEMS TOO MUCH MAKE ´EM BLEED
I FOUND A WAY
OUT OF THE DARK
LEAVING THIS WORLD JUST WITH MY HEART
FLYING AWAY

LEAVING THE EARTH AND FLYING AWAY
AS LONG AS I FLY I´M FEELING OK
LEAVING BEHIND MY BODY NOW
FLYING AWAY ALRIGHT SOMEHOW
LEAVING THIS PLACE
LEAVING THIS MESS
FOREVER NOW

P - R

PAPER PLANES

A ROSE IN MY HAND
FOR MY TRUE LOVING FRIEND
A RING SO UNIQUE
FOR THE MAN I JUST NEED

A KISS IN THE AIR
AND I KNOW YOU´LL BE THERE
A SMILE JUST FOR YOU
AS WE ARE GOING TO

A LAND PAPER PLANES
IN THE AIR EVERYWHERE
THE SWEET SOFTER RIDES
PAPER PLANES ARE ALL RIGHT
AND WE SMILE CAUSE WE KNOW
IT´S ALRIGHT

A ROAR IN THE NIGHT
YES, WE FEEL QUITE ALL RIGHT
A SCREAM IN THE DARK
AND SO FAST THUMPS MY HEART

IN A LAND PAPER PLANES
IN THE AIR EVERYWHERE
THE SWEET SOFTER RIDES
PAPER PLANES ARE ALL RIGHT
AND WE SMILE CAUSE WE KNOW
IT´S ALRIGHT

PARTY TIL THE LIGHT

AS I TURN AROUND THIS CORNER
I JUST KNOW I´LL HAVE A NIGHT OF FUN
HANDSOME IN MY DARKEST SMOKING
I´M ON THE RUN

ENTRANCE HAS A GOLDEN CARPET
AS I PAY A-HUNDRED FOR THE NIGHT
ROUND ME ARE THE SEXY LADIES
IN HOT RED LIGHT

BLONDE ONE TAKES ME BY THE HAND
I CLOSE MY EYES
AND FEEL HER LIPS EVERYWHERE
RED ONE CAUGHT ME BY SURPRISE
SHE LIKES MY SIZE
I FEEL HER HANDS EVERYWHERE
I ENJOY THIS NIGHT
PARTY TIL THE LIGHT

I CAN´T TELL YOU ALL THE DETAILS
BUT BELIEVE ME I´M A LUCKY BLOKE
I CAN HAVE A BIG EXPERIENCE
DOWN ON THE ROAD

THAT´S WHY I´M RIGHT ON MY WAY TO
PARADISE, I´M COMING AFTER YOU
ROUND ME ALL THE SEXY LADIES
I PREFER NEW

LAILA TAKES ME BY THE HAND
I CLOSE MY EYES
AND FEEL HER LIPS EVERYWHERE
AMY CAUGHT ME BY SURPRISE
SHE LIKES MY SIZE
I FEEL HER HANDS EVERYWHERE
I ENJOY THIS NIGHT
PARTY TIL THE LIGHT

PERCY PRINGLE´S HOUSE OF LOVE

I TAKE YOU TO THE JUNGLE
OF HATE AND GREEDY LIES
TO FIND OUT THE CHARACTER OF YOU
AND THERE IS PERCY PRINGLE
THE THIRD OF IN A LINE
HE´S HERE JUST TO FIND OUT IF YOU´RE TRUE

IN PERCY PRINGLE´S HOUSE OF LOVE
HE TAKES CONTROL OF ALL YOUR MEMORIES
JUST CLOSE YOUR EYES AND LET IT OUT
UNTIL THE DAY HE KNOWS YOUR FANTASIES
THE ONE YOU´RE ON YOUR KNEES
INCLUDING ME

BEFORE I MAKE YOU HAPPY
BEFORE YOU BREAK ME DOWN
I NEED ALL THE REASONS IN YOUR MIND
DON´T TELL ME THAT I´M CRAZY
I´M NOT A SILLY CLOWN
I NEED ALL THE HINTS I CANNOT FIND

IN PERCY PRINGLE´S HOUSE OF LOVE
HE TAKES CONTROL OF ALL YOUR MEMORIES
JUST CLOSE YOUR EYES AND LET IT OUT
UNTIL THE DAY HE KNOWS YOUR FANTASIES
THE ONE YOU´RE ON YOUR KNEES
INCLUDING ME

DOWN YOUR THROAT AND IN THE SKY
WHERE DEADLY GHOSTS ARE HAUNTING ME
I MUST KNOW YOU´RE FULL OF LIGHT
AND LOVE FOR ME

PERFECT STRANGER
(SONIC TEARS)

SEE YOU THERE AND TALK
TO ANOTHER HANDSOME DREAMER IN THE DARK
WATCH YOU SHAKE AND SMILE
AS THE GUY IS COMING CLOSER NEAR TO YOU

SONIC TEARS
ROLLING DOWN INTO MY FACE
ONE MORE BEER
WATCHING ON WITH DEEP DISGRACE

AS THE SCENE IS TURNING
OUR LOVE GETS FAR AWAY
AND MY HEART IS BURNING
I AM CRYING FOR A DAY
HE´S THE PERFECT STRANGER
AND YOUR EYES ARE ALL ON HIM
HE´S THE PERFECT DANGER
AS MY ICE FEELS VERY THIN

THOUGHT YOU´D BE MY ONE
OUT OF ALL THE PRETTY LADIES IN THE SUN
NEVER KNEW THE TRUTH
NOW I SEE YOUR ALL BUT HONEST BREAKING NEWS

CRUEL´S THE WORLD
SEEMS YOU REALLY JUST DON´T CARE
CAUSE I FEEL
SEXY TIMES ARE IN THE AIR

NOW THE SCENE IS TURNING
AND OUR LOVE GETS FAR AWAY
AND MY HEART IS BURNING
I AM CRYING FOR A DAY
HE´S THE PERFECT STRANGER
AND YOUR EYES ARE ALL ON HIM
HE´S THE PERFECT DANGER
AS MY ICE FEELS VERY THIN

PLAYBOY, SUPERSTAR AND SUPERFLY

I LIVE FOR ETERNITY
MONEY, GIRLS AND FAME
FIRE HOT MY CHEMISTRY
I KNOW TO PLAY THE GAME

IN THOUSANDS OF YEARS
I´M STILL IN YOUR EARS
CAUSE THE MASTER OF GAMES
WILL BE FAMOUS IN NAMES

MR. SUPERSTAR - PLAYBOY IN HIS CAR
MR. SUPERFLY - HIGHWAY PATROLLING I
HANDSOME AND GOOD IS MY WORK AS A LOVE MACHINE
GIRLS START TO CRY
WHEN I LEAVE THEIR PATHETIC DREAM
I´M A SUPERSTAR - FAMOUS IN MY CAR
SUCH A SUPERFLY - FLYING UP TO THE SKY
1000 GIRLS WILL BE MINE IN A LONELY YEAR
GIRLS FLYING HIGH AS I TAKE THEM AWAY FROM HERE

I WAS BORN A SELFISH MAN
DADDY WAS A FOOL
PLAYING GAMES WITH MANY NAMES
LEAVING OUT EVERY RULE

THEN WHEN I WAS 10
HE MADE ME A MAN
I BECAME WHO I AM
THAT´S BECAUSE I JUST CAN

I´M A SUPERSTAR - FAMOUS IN MY CAR
SUCH A SUPERFLY - FLYING UP TO THE SKY
1000 GIRLS WILL BE MINE IN A LONELY YEAR
GIRLS FLYING HIGH AS I TAKE THEM AWAY FROM HERE
MR. SUPERSTAR - PLAYBOY IN HIS CAR
MR. SUPERFLY - HIGHWAY PATROLLING I
HANDSOME AND GOOD IS MY WORK AS A LOVE MACHINE
GIRLS START TO CRY
WHEN I LEAVE THEIR PATHETIC DREAM

POWER MONSTER

SEEING YOU IN SLEEP AROUND THIS DAY
DON'T KNOW WHY YOU'RE TIRED ALL THE WAY
DREAMING OF A LAND SO FAR AWAY
WHERE YOU CAN RELAX AND THERE YOU STAY

LOOK INTO MY EYES, I'M PRETTY STRONG
WORKING ALL AROUND THE CLOCK AND ON
I'M THE POWER MONSTER JUST FOR YOU
I'M THE POWER MONSTER CAUSE OF YOU

I GET UP AT 5 AND COME BACK LATE
IF YOU CAN I PAY A DINNER DATE
BUT FOR SURE YOU ARE TOO TIRED NOW
I CLEAN UP THE FLOOR, THE BATHROOM NOW

LOOK INTO MY EYES, I'M PRETTY STRONG
WORKING ALL AROUND THE CLOCK AND ON
I'M THE POWER MONSTER JUST FOR YOU
I'M THE POWER MONSTER CAUSE OF YOU

I DON'T KNOW HOW YOU SPEND YOUR DAY
THERE'S SO MUCH TIME YOU SLEEP AWAY
MAYBE YOU CHANGE BEFORE I DIE
THERE'S SOMETHING MORE THAT YOU SHOULD TRY

WORKING JUST FOR TWO, THIS IS MY LIFE
MONSTER POWER MAN, I FEEL ALIVE
GIVING YOU MY LOVE WHILE YOU'RE ASLEEP
IS IT REALLY NICE YOU'RE SUCH A CHEAT?

PROOVE YOURSELF RIGHT

LOOK INTO MY EYES
AND TELL ME THE SAME OLD STORY
YESTERDAY AWAY
THE COMPANY NEEDED YOU
I´M AT HOME ALONE A-WAITIN´ FOR 20 HOURS
I´M TRYIN´ TO BELIEVE IT´S TRUE

LOOK INTO MY EYES
AND TELL ME I´M SO MISTAKEN
THE RUMOURS I JUST HEARD
ARE NOTHING BUT PLAIN OLD LIES
IF YOU SHOW ME JUST ONE SIGN OF LOVIN´
I COULD BELIEVE IT OR OTHER WAY I SYMPATHIZE

SHOW ME A WAY OUT OF YOUR DARK
PROOVE YOURSELF RIGHT AND IF YOU CAN
WE CAN TRY ANOTHER START
I WILL BE CLOSE TO YOU AGAIN
OTHERWISE, GIRL, I´M AWAY
PROOVING YOU WRONG I´LL LET YOU GO
NEVER AGAIN WILL I STAY, PLAYING IN THIS SCENARIO
LOSING MY LIFE AND RUN AWAY INTO THE DAY

LOOK INTO MY EYES
AND TELL ME YOU´RE EYES AIN´T LYING
ONCE UP EVERY WEEK
YOU LIVE IT UP ON YOUR OWN
MAYBE I´M A FOOL BUT MAYBE YOU MAKE ME CRYING
YOU TREAT ME LIKE A ROLLING STONE

SHOW ME A WAY OUT OF YOUR DARK
PROOVE YOURSELF RIGHT AND IF YOU CAN
WE CAN MAKE ANOTHER START
I WILL BE CLOSE TO YOU AGAIN
OTHERWISE, GIRL, I´M AWAY
PROOVING YOU WRONG I´LL LET YOU GO
NEVER AGAIN WILL I STAY, PLAYING IN THIS SCENARIO
LOSING MY LIFE AND RUN AWAY INTO THE DAY

PURPLE EYES

AS I SEE YOUR PURPLE EYES
I JUST KNOW MY LOVE IS OVER NOW
CAUGHT YOUR PICTURE BY SURPRISE
BUT I KNEW MY LOVE IS OVER NOW
SAID GOODBYE TO ALL MY LIFE
THOUGH I´M SORRY FOR MY WIFE

SAW THIS PAIR OF PURPLE EYES
I KNEW SOMEONE HAD TO PAY THE PRICE
LEFT MY WIFE FOR BIG SURPRISE
CAUSE SHE DIDN´T HAVE SOME PURPLE EYES
LEFT MY HOUSE AND ALL THE CARS
GAVE MY LIFE UP TO THE STARS

THE MAGIC OF YOUR PURPLE EYES
IT IS STRONGER THAN A SACK OF GOLD
I CAUGHT YOUR PICTURE BY SURPRISE
AND I HAD TO MOVE BEFORE I´M OLD
NOW I´M FEELING LIKE A MAN
SO DELICIOUS TIL THE END

STILL I DON´T KNOW MUCH OF YOU
BUT I´M HAPPY WITH YOU BY MY SIDE
EVERYTHING YOU WANNA DO
I´M WITH YOU AND KISS YOUR PURPLE EYES
ALL MY LIFE WAS NOT THE SAME
NOW THE SUNSHINE EATS THE RAIN

THE MAGIC OF YOUR PURPLE EYES
IT IS STRONGER THAN A SACK OF GOLD
I CAUGHT YOUR PICTURE BY SURPRISE
AND I HAD TO MOVE BEFORE I´M OLD
NOW I´M FEELING LIKE A MAN
SO DELICIOUS TIL THE END

QUEEN OF MINE

AM I RIGHT? AM I WRONG?
IS IT REALLY TRUE YOU´RE MOVING ON?
ARE YOU CRUEL? ARE YOU NICE?
HOTTER THAN THE SUN OR COLD AS ICE?

WAKING UP WITH YOU IN MY HEAD
EMPTY IN MY COLD LITTLE BED

QUEEN OF MINE
DON´T KNOW IF YOU CARE ´BOUT MY LOVE
IF YOU DO
COME BACK AND EXPERIENCE MY LOVE
YESTERDAY
YOU AND I WERE PERFECTLY ONE
COME AND STAY
AS I FEEL MY LOVE IS SO STRONG

CURLY BLONDE, CURLY WHITE
SEXY, WHAT A SMILE, I SAW THE LIGHT
HANDS IN RINGS, LEGS IN SHAPE
ASKED YOU FOR A RICH HOT DINNER DATE

AFTERWARDS WE CAME VERY CLOSE
KISSED YOU ON YOUR LIPS AND YOUR NOSE

QUEEN OF MINE
DON´T KNOW IF YOU CARE ´BOUT MY LOVE
IF YOU DO
COME BACK AND EXPERIENCE MY LOVE
YESTERDAY
YOU AND I WERE PERFECTLY ONE
COME AND STAY
AS I FEEL MY LOVE IS SO STRONG

RABBIT SWEET

ESTABLISHED '91
AND TRUSTED AS REALLY GOOD
A TOY OF JOY AND FUN
ESPECIALLY FOR GOOD MOOD
IT´S A THING
YOU ALL PLAY IN THE DARK
CAN´T YOU THINK
YOU´RE ALONE IN YOUR HEART?

GRAVITY IS NEARLY FALLING APART
HONESTLY I WATCHED AND LEARNED
FROM THE SHARK
A RABBIT SWEET, A RABBIT NICE
MY RABBIT SHOWS YOU PARADISE
IT´S GAINING FAST, YOU´RE FLYING HIGH
EMOTION´S STRONG, ANOTHER CRY
USE IT NOW AGAIN
BETTER AS A MAN

I STUDIED DR. HOUSE
AND FOLLOWED UP MURPHY´S LAW
I TRIED WITH HANDS AND MOUTH
BUT MOST OF THEM CAME NO MORE
THAT´S WHEN I FOUND A WAY
TO BE KING
WITH THIS THING IN MY HANDS
I´M YOUR KING

GRAVITY IS NEARLY FALLING APART
HONESTLY I WATCHED AND LEARNED
FROM THE SHARK
A RABBIT SWEET, A RABBIT NICE
MY RABBIT SHOWS YOU PARADISE
IT´S GAINING FAST, YOU´RE FLYING HIGH
EMOTION´S STRONG, ANOTHER CRY
USE IT NOW AGAIN
BETTER AS A MAN

RIESENMOND

DER RIESENMOND GEHT VORBEI
DIE BLUMEN WELKEN NICHT
UND SETZEN LIEBE FREI
GLÜCKSHORMONE FÜR UNS ZWEI

TRÄNEN LÜGEN NICHT, SCHAU IN MEIN GESICHT
UND DIE SONNE KOMMT ANS LICHT

WILLST DU REISEN DURCH DIE WELT
ZUSAMMEN NUR MIT MIR?
VON NORDEN NACH SÜDEN
WILLST DU RIESENMONDE SEHEN?
DURCH ZAUBERWÄLDER GEHEN?

KOMM UND LASS UNS STARTEN JETZT
RIESENMONDE SIND NICHT VERHEXT
LEINEN LOS UND ANGEGAST
RIESENMONDE SIND NICHT ABGEGRAST

AB INS ABENDROT WO DIE LIEBE WOHNT
EINE PAUSE NUR FÜR UNS
NUR DER RIESENMOND IST HEUT NACHT BEWOHNT
ER LEUCHTET STÄRKER ALS ALLE STERNE GLÜHEN

WILLST DU REISEN DURCH DIE WELT
ZUSAMMEN NUR MIT MIR?
VON NORDEN NACH SÜDEN
WILLST DU RIESENMONDE SEHEN?
DURCH ZAUBERWÄLDER GEHEN HEUT NACHT?

KURZ VORM ZIEL WIRD ES DÜSTER
IST ES SCHON VORBEI ODER EIN TRAUM?
DER RIESENMOND KLAPPT AUF UND BRICHT ENTZWEI
ER EXPLODIERT, ER GIBT UNS FREI

ALL DIE LIEBE DIE WIR GERADE SPÜREN
SIE IST TIEF BEWEGEND UND SCHENKT UNS KRAFT
DAS FEUERWERK LEUCHTET HELL
NUR FÜR UNS

ROCKIN´ REBEL

DIDN´T KNOW THE WORD OF TURNING
MOVING ON, MY HEAD IS BURNING
LEAVING YOU BEHIND, MY ANGEL
LEAVING YOU BEHIND, FORGET YOU
WE HAD SUCH A TIME OF GLORY
EVERYTHING WE HAD, OUR STORY
COULDN´T CARRY ON, I´M LEAVING
RIGHT INTO A WORLD OF GIVING

WHEN I WAS A LITTLE BABY
DREAMING OF A PRETTY LADY
LOOKING FOR A PERFECT BODY
SEXY BABY, PRETTY NAUGHTY
THEN I SAW YOU IN A CORNER
DANCING TO MISS TINA TURNER
WHEN OUR EYES THEN SAW EACH OTHER
TALKING, DANCING, I´M YOUR LOVER

TAKE IT TO ANOTHER LEVEL, I WAS BORN A ROCKIN´ REBEL
SPRINGSTEEN, HENDRIX AND MADONNA
I´M THE PRINCE OF LITTLE PERSIA
LOOKING FOR A PRETTY LADY
TAKE HER AS MY NEWEST BABY
I WAS BORN A ROCKIN´ REBEL, TAKE IT TO ANOTHER LEVEL

SOMETHING, SOMEWHERE, SOMEONE TELL ME
IS IT RIGHT TO CHANGE THE RALLYE?
MOVING ON INSTEAD OF STAYING
LOOKING FOR ANOTHER LADY
NOW THAT I´M A ROCKIN´ REBEL
TAKE IT TO A DIFFERENT LEVEL
RIGHT INTO YOUR ARMS I´M DANCING
STRAIGHT INTO A NEW ROMANCING

TAKE IT TO ANOTHER LEVEL, I WAS BORN A ROCKIN´ REBEL
SPRINGSTEEN, HENDRIX AND MADONNA
I´M THE PRINCE OF LITTLE PERSIA
LOOKING FOR A PRETTY LADY
TAKE HER AS MY NEWEST BABY
I WAS BORN A ROCKIN´ REBEL, TAKE IT TO ANOTHER LEVEL

ROMEO IN JUNE

ROMEO THE MAN IS HERE TO GIVE
JULIA A KISS OF LOVE
BODIES YOUNG AND SWEET UNITE
TO THE STARS ABOVE

ROMEO THE MAN IS HERE TO LIVE
SUCH A LIFE OF FUN AND JOY
JULIA´S THE QUEEN
AND ROMEO IS HER BOY

HANDS THEY UNITE AGAIN
UNDERNEATH THE MOON
LIPS FEEL SO FREE AGAIN
ROMEO IN JUNE
LOVE IN THE AIR JUST FOR THIS PRETTY SCENE
MAGICAL STARS BELIEVE TO SHINE
MAKE IT ALL UP
JUST FOR THIS SPECIAL DREAM OF MINE

REMEO THE MAN IS HERE TO KISS
JULIA OF 21
SHOWING HER A LOVE OF TENDERNESS
AND GOOD FUN

ROMEO THE MAN IS HERE TO MAKE
FEELINGS REALLY STRONG AGAIN
JULIA ENJOYS
CUTE ROMEO IS HER MAN

HANDS THEY UNITE AGAIN
UNDERNEATH THE MOON
LIPS FEEL SO FREE AGAIN
ROMEO IN JUNE
LOVE IN THE AIR JUST FOR THIS PRETTY SCENE
MAGICAL STARS BELIEVE TO SHINE
MAKE IT ALL UP
JUST FOR THIS SPECIAL DREAM OF MINE

RUNNING AWAY FROM YOU

AS IT´S TIME TO FORGIVE
ALL THE UGLY THINGS YOU WERE BORN TO GIVE
DAY AND NIGHT, NIGHT AND DAY
ALL YOUR EVIL THOUGHTS THEY WON´T GO AWAY
BETTER LEAVE ME ALONE TO SAVE MY DAY

A SEA OF SHADOWS BEHIND MY BACK
DREAMING OF LOVE INSANITY
A FLAME OF SADNESS FOR THIS AND THAT
LEAVE ME ALONE
LEAVING MY HOME

I START TO SHIVER AND NOW I CRY
I´M RUNNING AWAY FROM YOU
I SEE THE THOUGHTS IN YOUR MIND AND FLY
I´M LEAVING INTO THE BLUE
I´M RUNNING AWAY FROM YOU

NO MORE TIME TO FORGIVE
ALL THE CHANCES YOU HAD, THE LIFE YOU LIVE
SO OBSCURE, SO DERANGED
I BELIEVE IN YOU BUT YOU NEVER CHANGE
ALL THE THINGS IN YOUR MIND ARE VERY STRANGE

INSTEAD OF PLAYING SOME FRIENDS OF FUN
GIVING SOME LOVE AND TENDERNESS
YOU STILL PREFER NOW TO KILL THE SUN
LIVING YOUR WAY
RUINING MY DAY

I START TO SHIVER AND NOW I CRY
I´M RUNNING AWAY FROM YOU
I SEE THE THOUGHTS IN YOUR MIND AND FLY
I´M LEAVING INTO THE BLUE
I´M RUNNING AWAY FROM YOU

S - U

SANDRA

SANDRA, YOU´RE THE ONE
3 YEARS AND SO ON
WE´RE A PAIR UNTIL WE LEAVE THIS WORLD

EVEN THEN I´M SURE
WE ARE OUT FOR MORE
HAND IN HAND WITH YOU, MY PRETTY GIRL

LOOK IN MY EYES
AND HEAR MY WORDS
WE FLY AWAY
LIKE PRETTY BIRDS

SANDRA, I MISS YOU WHEN AWAY
OH SANDRA, I KISS YOU EVERY DAY
I´M SO IN LOVE
SANDRA, YOUR HANDS UPON MY CHEST
SANDRA, WITH YOU I LIVE MY BEST
SUNSHINE MY FACE, SUNSHINE MY DAYS

WAKE AND MAKE ME SMILE
EVERY DAY AND MILE
SIDE BY SIDE WE FLY THROUGH OUR LIVES

EVEN WHEN WE´RE SAD
FIGHTING BEING MAD
OUR LOVE IS STRONGER THAN THE DRIVES

FROM DAY TO DAY
FROM YEAR TO YEAR
I LOVE YOU MORE
SANDRA, MY DEAR

SANDRA, FROM NOW UNTIL THE END
OH SANDRA, I HOLD YOUR LOVIN´ HAND
DON´T LET YOU GO
SANDRA, I LOVE YOU EVERY DAY
SANDRA, I LOVE YOU EVERY WAY
HOLD ME AGAIN, YOUR LOVIN´ MAN

155

SANDRA GOODBYE

MAGICAL MOMENTS FROM THE PAST
I TURN AROUND TO BE YOUR GUEST
SO MANY FACES FULL OF JOY
MAKING ME FEEL A YOUNGER BOY

AND I SEE THE SWEETEST GIRL I KNOW
HAND IN HAND, THE TIME WAS GREAT, YOU GO
SANDRA AND I, ONE MORE TRY
SANDRA GOODBYE, NOW I CRY

LYING IN BED BEFORE I DIE
CALLING THE PEOPLE OF MY LIFE
SUDDENLY SOMEONE´S AT THE DOOR
FEELING MY HEART CAN´T TAKE NO MORE

AND I SEE THE SWEETEST GIRL I KNOW
HAND IN HAND, THE TIME WAS GREAT, I GO
SANDRA AND I, ONE MORE TRY
SANDRA GOODBYE, NOW I DIE

SCARY SHADOWS I LIKE

10 PEOPLE IN A LITTLE ROOM
NOT WORKING NOR ARE THEY FREE
THE STRONG ARE GETTING CRAZY SOON
THE WEAK ALREADY IN TEARS

THEY TRY TO FIND A DOOR
THEY TRY TO FIGHT SOME MORE

I SWITCH AND TURN OFF THE LIGHT
I HEAR THEM SCREAM FOR PARADISE
THEY FIGHT THE HORROR INSIDE
I MAKE 'EM BLEED
FOR ALL THEIR STUPID LIES
SCARY SHADOWS I LIKE
I'M A DEVIL TONIGHT
AND YOU'RE OUT

I KNEW I HAD ANOTHER CHOICE
BUT NO, SIR, I DIDN'T CARE
EACH ONE OF ALL THE HELPLESS GUYS
WAS LOOKING DOWN ON ME THERE

THE LADIES TURNED AWAY
AND NOW I MAKE MY DAY

I SWITCH AND TURN OFF THE LIGHT
I HEAR THEM SCREAM FOR PARADISE
THEY FIGHT THE HORROR INSIDE
I MAKE 'EM BLEED
FOR ALL THEIR STUPID LIES
SCARY SHADOWS I LIKE
I'M A DEVIL TONIGHT
AND YOU'RE OUT

SCHENK MIR EINE NEUE NACHT MIT DIR
(PRINZ VON LIECHTENSTEIN)

DIE SEHNSUCHT RUFT NACH ZÄRTLICHKEIT
UND ICH RUF DICH AN
DAS LETZTE MAL MIT DIR IM ARM
WAR IRGENDWANN

ICH BIN DER PRINZ VON LIECHTENSTEIN
UND TRÄUME VON DIR
KÜSS MICH ZART UND HALT MICH FEST
GANZ NAH BEI MIR

SCHENK MIR EINE NEUE NACHT MIT DIR
VOLLER LIEBE UND MEHR
EINE BLUME VOLLER ZÄRTLICHKEIT
WIE EIN FLAMMENDES MEER
EINE NACHT MIT PRINZ VON LIECHTENSTEIN
VOLLER LIEBE UND GLÜCK
SCHENK MIR EINE NEUE NACHT MIT DIR
UND KOMM ZU MIR ZURÜCK

DER MAGEN KNURRT, EIN GAUMENSCHMAUS
VON JIM FÜR UNS ZWEI
EIN RENDEZVOUS BEI KERZENSCHEIN
UND EDLEM WEIN

DEIN ABENDKLEID, EIN HAUCH VON NICHTS
KOMM, STOSS MIT MIR AN
MIT DEM PRINZ VON LIECHTENSTEIN
IN EDLEM GEWAND

SCHENK MIR EINE NEUE NACHT MIT DIR
VOLLER LIEBE UND MEHR
EINE BLUME VOLLER ZÄRTLICHKEIT
WIE EIN FLAMMENDES MEER
EINE NACHT MIT PRINZ VON LIECHTENSTEIN
VOLLER LIEBE UND GLÜCK
SCHENK MIR EINE NEUE NACHT MIT DIR
UND KOMM ZU MIR ZURÜCK

SEHNSUCHT

SEHNSUCHT HEISST DER ORT
AN DEM ICH EINSAM STEH
DIE LIEBE DIE IST FORT
ES TUT IMMER NOCH SEHR WEH

KOMM UND LADE MICH EIN
AUF DIE INSEL IM PARADIES
DORT WO ALLES SICH LIEBT
DORT WO EINSAMKEIT WIRD BESIEGT

ICH SEHNE MICH
ICH LECHZE NUR NACH DIR
DU SIEHST MICH AN
UND KOMMST GANZ SCHNELL ZU MIR
EIN POTPOURRI DER LIEBE
SPIELT EIN LIED
ICH BIN SO FROH
DASS ES DICH WIRKLICH GIBT

SEHNSUCHT HEISST DER ORT
AN DEM ICH EINSAM STAND
DIE LIEBE DIE WAR FORT
GING NACH EINFACH UNBEKANNT

DOCH ICH STECKTE NICHT AUF
LIESS DEM SCHICKSALSWEG SEINEN LAUF
DU STANDST PLÖTZTLICH VOR MIR
UND ICH TRÄUMTE NUR NOCH VON DIR

ICH SEHNE MICH
ICH LECHZE NUR NACH DIR
DU SIEHST MICH AN
UND KOMMST GANZ SCHNELL ZU MIR
EIN POTPOURRI DER LIEBE
SPIELT EIN LIED
ICH BIN SO FROH
DASS ES DICH WIRKLICH GIBT

SEXY IN RED

SEXY IN RED
THIS GIRL IS NEARLY SMILING FROM BED TO BED
SHALL I BECOME
ANOTHER SIMPLE ONE WHO BELIEVES IN FUN?

I´M JUST A BOY WITH OPEN EYES
AND SOME DREAMS
THIS SEXY RED IS WHAT SHE SEEMS

CURTAIN CALLS
AND IN MY VELVET BED WE FEEL ALRIGHT
SEXY GIRL
AND I JUST TAKE THE DAY INTO THE NIGHT
DEVIL SMILES
CAUSE ALL THE SEXY LINES ARE IN MY EYES
LOVE IS NICE
BUT MAKING LOVE IS HAVING BETTER TIMES

SEXY IN RED
A NAUGHTY GIRL OF 18 IS IN MY BED
I´M NOT THE FIRST
SO MANY MEN BEFORE ME, I´M NOT THE LAST

WHEN I AM OLDER IN THE GREY
OR THE BLUE
I WILL FOR SURE REMEMBER YOU

CURTAIN CALLS
AND IN MY VELVET BED WE FEEL ALRIGHT
SEXY GIRL
AND I JUST TAKE THE DAY INTO THE NIGHT
DEVIL SMILES
CAUSE ALL THE SEXY LINES ARE IN MY EYES
LOVE IS NICE
BUT MAKING LOVE IS HAVING BETTER TIMES

SEXY SHADOW

I´M WALKING DOWN THAT CRAZY ROAD
THOUGH STICKS AND STONES MAY BREAK MY BONES
NO TURNING BACK, I LEAVE BEHIND
WHAT´S IN MY MIND, I NEED TO FIND

ANOTHER LOVE FOR ME AND YOU
WELL, THIS IS TRUE, I´VE GOT NO CLUE
IF I WILL FIND THE SPECIAL ONE
TO REACH THE SUN

SOME BUTTERFLIES AROUND ME AS THE END IS NEAR
THE STONY ROAD TURNS INTO GREEN
THE TULIPS ALL AROUND THEY SING A SONG OF LOVE
IT FEELS A DREAM
AND THERE´S A SEXY SHADOW COMING CLOSER NOW
HER PRETTY FACE TURNS INTO LIFE
HER SPARKLING LIPS AND PRETTY LEGS
JUST MAKE ME FLY, I´M SO ALIVE

I KNOW YOU MADE ENOUGH MISTAKES
AND SO DID I, WE REALLY TRIED
BUT TIME AND LIFE TOOK US APART
IT BROKE MY HEART, YOU BROKE MY HEART

SO I DECIDED TO BE TRUE
WAS LEAVING YOU INTO THE BLUE
TO FIND ANOTHER ONE FOR ME
AND NOW I SEE

SOME BUTTERFLIES AROUND ME AS THE END IS NEAR
THE STONY ROAD TURNS INTO GREEN
THE TULIPS ALL AROUND THEY SING A SONG OF LOVE
IT FEELS A DREAM
AND THERE´S A SEXY SHADOW COMING CLOSER NOW
HER PRETTY FACE TURNS INTO LIFE
HER SPARKLING LIPS AND PRETTY LEGS
JUST MAKE ME FLY, I´M SO ALIVE

SHIFT INTO PARADISE

A LOVE WAS NEVER GOOD ENOUGH FOR ME
I´VE TRIED MY BEST AND REACHED FOR THE STARS
UNTIL THE DAY
YOUR BEAUTY BLOWING ME AWAY

I´VE NEVER SEEN A GIRL LIKE YOU BEFORE
YOUR SMILE CAN END THE WAR GAMES FOR SURE
YOU ARE A LIGHT
THE DARKNESS NEEDS TO FEEL TONIGHT

A SPECIAL DAY OF MAGIC COMES ALIVE
I TURN AROUND AND SHIFT INTO PARADISE
I´VE NEVER BEEN SO HAPPY IN MY LIFE
YOU LIFT IT UP BUT MAYBE THINKING OTHERWISE
COULD ALL THIS SCENE BE FANTASY UNREAL?
BUT FOR A LIE MY FEELINGS ARE SO REAL
YOUR LOVE I FEEL

I´VE TRIED TO FIND THE ONE AND ONLY LOVE
BUT TEARS OF SADNESS FELL DOWN ON ME
A STUPID WORLD
SO HOPELESS, DIDN´T FIND MY GIRL

BUT LIFE WAS GOOD BEFORE MY BREAKING DOWN
I FOUND YOU AS YOU´RE COMING MY WAY
A SHOOTING STAR
IS FLYING RIGHT INTO MY ARM

A SPECIAL DAY OF MAGIC COMES ALIVE
I TURN AROUND AND SHIFT INTO PARADISE
I´VE NEVER BEEN SO HAPPY IN MY LIFE
YOU LIFT IT UP BUT MAYBE THINKING OTHERWISE
COULD ALL THIS SCENE BE FANTASY UNREAL?
BUT FOR A LIE MY FEELINGS ARE SO REAL
YOUR LOVE I FEEL

SMS
(NO MORE LOVE)

SMS ON ONE DAY
I JUST FELT WE´RE OK
SMS MADE ME CRY
OUR LOVE HAS JUST DIED AGAIN

NO MORE, NO MORE LOVE
FIGHT AGAIN FOR ANOTHER LOVE
DULL AND COLD´S YOUR HEART
NO MORE LOVE

SMS KILLED MY HEART
WASHED MY BRAIN, MADE US PART
NEARLY 4 HAPPY YEARS
WE JUST HAD, I´M IN TEARS AGAIN

NO MORE, NO MORE LOVE
FIGHT AGAIN FOR ANOTHER LOVE
DULL AND COLD´S YOUR HEART
NO MORE LOVE
FIGHT AGAIN FOR ANOTHER START
FOR ANOTHER HEART, ON AGAIN

SPECIAL GRAVY TRAIN

GRAVY TRAINS
MOVE IN INTO THE NIGHT
RAINY TRAINS
HEADING ON TO A LIGHT
CITY TRAINS
THEY MAKE ME FEEL ALRIGHT

GAINING SPEED
AND LOSING CONTROL
IN THE HEAT
HE´S READY TO ROLL
FEEL THE BEAT
AND LOSING NOW CONTROL

THE SPECIAL GRAVY TRAIN IN THE HEAT OF THE NIGHT
FROM A TO B TO C, CALLING OUT FOR A LIGHT
IT´S LIKE A NEON TRAIN, FACE IS SHINY IN BLUE
SO CAN YOU FEEL IT NOW?
THE TRAIN IS COMING THROUGH

TAKE IT DOWN
TRAIN IS ROARING AWAY
MAKE IT NOW
SUCH A TRIP IN A DAY
HOLY COW
THE PEOPLE ARE SO GAY

MONSTER TRAIN
LOOKING LIKE OUT OF HELL
GRAVY TRAIN
WITH A DUSTY OLD BELL
RISE TO FAME
HE´S RIDING PRETTY WELL

THE SPECIAL GRAVY TRAIN IN THE HEAT OF THE NIGHT
FROM A TO B TO C, CALLING OUT FOR A LIGHT
IT´S LIKE A NEON TRAIN, FACE IS SHINY IN BLUE
SO CAN YOU FEEL IT NOW?
THE TRAIN IS COMING THROUGH

SPIEL AUF MEINER ZAUBERFLÖTE

ES IST SAMSTAGABEND
ICH FLIRTE DICH AN
DU SUCHST DIR HEUT NACHT 'NEN MANN
ICH BIN DER BESTE
DEN DU JE BEKOMMST
ICH ZEIG DIR WAS ICH SO KANN

DENN ICH ZÄHM DICH
BIS DU VOR MIR KNIEST
UND AUF MEINER
ZAUBERFLÖTE SPIELST
DER COUNTDOWN LÄUFT

DU KASSIERST DIE QUITTUNG
DU TUST ES SO GERN
STEIL HEB ICH AB ZU 'NEM STERN
NACH DEM RODEO
BRAUCHST DU EINEN DRINK
DU TRINKST 'NEN WHISKY MIT GIN

UND ICH ZÄHM DICH
BIS DU VOR MIR KNIEST
UND AUF MEINER
ZAUBERFLÖTE SPIELST
DER COUNTDOWN LÄUFT

DIESE UNSERE NACHT IST SO GENIAL
SPIEL DIE ZAUBERFLÖTE JETZT NOCHMAL

IMMER WIEDER
SPÜR ICH DICH AN MIR
DEINE HÄNDE
SPIELEN AUF MIR KLAVIER
ICH TRINK MEIN BIER

SPINNING WHEELS UP IN MY HEAD

NOWHERE IN TIME
LIVING ALONE
ALL OF MY LIFE
BROTHER IS DEAD
SISTER IS GONE
GIRLFRIEND GOODBYE

HEAVEN ON EARTH
DARKNESS OUTSIDE
I AM ALONE
LIVING MY LIFE
SLEEPING ALL DAY
I SHOULD HAVE KNOWN

THE SPICKS AND SPECKS WERE HAUNTING ME
AND SPINNING WHEELS ARE AFTER ME
I TRIED TO RUN, I HEARD A VOICE
SO LONG AGO
DOWN IN MY CHAIR I CLOSE MY EYES
I TRY TO LIVE IN PARADISE
THE SPICKS AND SPECKS, THE SPINNING WHEELS
UP IN MY HEAD

TAKING SOME PILLS
TAKING A DRINK
FADING AWAY
DREAMING A DREAM
FEELING SO REAL
WHAT CAN I SAY?

THE SPICKS AND SPECKS THEY TOOK ME DOWN
AND SPINNING WHEELS PUSHED ME AROUND
I TRIED TO RUN, I HEARD A VOICE
SO LONG AGO
DOWN IN MY CHAIR I DREAMT A DREAM
I TRIED TO LIVE RIGHT IN BETWEEN
THE SPICKS AND SPECKS, THE SPINNING WHEELS
UP IN MY HEAD

SPY GAMES
(BE MY DEVIL TONIGHT)

SPY GAMES UP IN THE BEDROOM
SPY GAMES UP IN THE NIGHT
LOVE GAMES OF DEEP EMOTIONS
LOVE GAMES WITH ME TONIGHT
DON'T FEEL MISTRADED, BABY, YOU ARE A STAR!
MAKE ME ANOTHER HEAVEN
THEREFORE YOU'LL BE MY DEVIL, RECORD THE LINES

SPY GAMES, SOME CRAZY LOVE FRAMES
PLAYING THIS GAME WITH YOU
SPY GAMES, SOME RED HOT LOVE FLAMES
FUN TIMES I HAVE WITH YOU
SOME MIXED EMOTIONS, OCEANS OF LOVE AND JOY
SHOW ME YOUR WORLD OF MAGIC
FUN GAMES, IT AIN'T NO TRAGIC THE NIGHT GOES ON

MAGICAL NIGHT, BE MY DEVIL TONIGHT
TAKE OFF YOUR STRING, YOU'RE MY QUEEN, I'M YOUR KING
MAGICAL NIGHT, I'M A PLAYBOY TONIGHT
MIRROWS OF LOVE WHILE I CAN'T GET ENOUGH
THE GAMES I WANNA PLAY WITH YOU
ARE PLUS 18, SOME ARE REALLY NEW
NOW HOLD YOUR BREATH UNTIL THE MORNING LIGHT
AND DREAM AWAY

SPY GAMES WITH DIFFERENT LOVE NAMES
TRUST ME AND CLOSE YOUR EYES
SPY GAMES WITH SONIC HEAT WAVES
GIVE YOU A BIG SURPRISE
I'LL MAKE YOU HAPPY MAYBE NEXT NIGHT AGAIN
SHOW ME YOUR KIND OF MAGIC
YOU'RE CLOSE TO BEING PERFECT THIS NIGHT AGAIN

MAGICAL NIGHT, BE MY DEVIL TONIGHT
TAKE OFF YOUR STRING, YOU'RE MY QUEEN, I'M YOUR KING
MAGICAL NIGHT, I'M A PLAYBOY TONIGHT
MIRROWS OF LOVE WHILE I CAN'T GET ENOUGH
THE GAMES I WANNA PLAY WITH YOU
ARE PLUS 18, SOME ARE REALLY NEW
NOW HOLD YOUR BREATH UNTIL THE MORNING LIGHT
AND DREAM AWAY

SUNSHINE DEEP INSIDE MY HEART

A SONG OF LOVE
I WRITE FOR YOU
CAUSE YOU´RE MY BABY
THE ONE I REALLY LOVE
AND SINCE THAT DAY
YOU LOVE ME TOO
WE SHINE TOGETHER
JUST LIKE TWO PRETTY STARS

IT´S TIME FOR LOVE UNTIL WE DIE
KISS ME NOW AND KISS ME NOW AGAIN
AS WE DIVE INTO THE NIGHT

A SUNSHINE DEEP INSIDE MY HEART
MY WORLD IS BEAUTIFUL AND REALLY NICE
YOU MAKE ME LIVE IN PARADISE
I FOUND THIS LOVE I WASN´T LOOKING FOR
A SWEET SURPRISE

I PAID THE PRICE
SHE BROKE MY HEART
I KNOW YOU´RE DIFFERENT
I KNOW YOUR LOVE IS TRUE
I KISS YOU, GIRL
I LOVE YOU TOO
MY LIFE IS SPECIAL
SO SPECIAL NOW WITH YOU

I QUIT MY LIFE TO STAY WITH YOU
LOVELY KIDS ARE SOMETHING WE SHOULD TRY
I CAN MAKE YOUR BODY FLY

A SUNSHINE DEEP INSIDE MY HEART
MY WORLD IS BEAUTIFUL AND REALLY NICE
YOU MAKE ME LIVE IN PARADISE
I FOUND THIS LOVE I WASN´T LOOKING FOR
A SWEET SURPRISE

SUPERFRAU

ALS ICH 17 WAR
DA LIEBTE ICH DIE MONIKA
SPÄTER KAM IRENE
DANN DIE JULIA
NACH DER BLONDEN GABI
MUSSTE ICH MICH NEU FORMIEREN
UND DANN SAH ICH JOSEFINE
UND ES WAR UM MICH GESCHEHEN

AUGEN WIE EIN ADLER
TIEFE BLICKE WIE EIN PFAU
LIPPEN WIE EIN REHSPITZ
DU BIST MEINE SUPERFRAU
BEINE WIE EIN PANTHER
SCHLANKE HÜFTEN WIE EIN GNU
ICH BIN DER CHRIS
UND WER BIST DU?

7 JAHRE DIESE LIEBE
BIS SIE MICH VERLIESS
JOSEFINE, DU WARST
WIRKLICH ZUCKERSÜSS
100 MÄDELS SPÄTER
SEH ICH PLÖTZLICH DIESE FRAU
IST ES WIRKLICH JOSEFINE?
WAS SIE WILL WEISS ICH GENAU

AUGEN WIE EIN ADLER
TIEFE BLICKE WIE EIN PFAU
LIPPEN WIE EIN REHSPITZ
DU BIST MEINE SUPERFRAU
BEINE WIE EIN PANTHER
SCHLANKE HÜFTEN WIE EIN GNU
ICH BIN DER CHRIS
UND WER BIST DU?

SURVIVOR

THE DAY WAS LONG ENOUGH TO CALL THE BELL
I WORKED WITHOUT A BREAK
A HANDSOME SURVIVOR
MY LIFE WAS GOOD BUT ENDED UP IN HELL
THE FLAMES ARE GETTING HIGH
TOO HOT IS THE FIRE

SHE LEFT ME AND I HAD TO PAY
SHE LEFT AND BURNED MY LIFE INTO ASHES
TO PAY HER OUT I WORK ALL DAY
AND THEN I SAY:

MAY GOD TAKE CARE OF YOU AND LIGHTEN IT UP
THE THINGS YOU DID TO ME, YOU´RE MAKING ME HOT
BUT I´M A MAN RELIGIOUS IN LIFE
I CUT MY BEARD AND WASH MY PRISONER´S FACE
NEXT LIFE I´LL KICK YOU OUT AND UP INTO SPACE
I WON´T FORGET THE DAY OF THE KNIFE

THE DAY WAS HARD ENOUGH TO SIT AND CRY
BELIEVE ME I´M A MAN
BUT HURTING MY FEELINGS
WAS CLOSE ENOUGH TO THINK I HAVE TO DIE
I FIGHT THE CURSE AND WORK
FOR DIFFERENT SEE-THINGS

I SEE YOUR FACE AND GIVE A DAMN
UP IN THE SKY MY FATHER GETS CRAZY
HE WAS A RIGHTFUL WORKING MAN
I WORK AGAIN

MAY GOD TAKE CARE OF YOU AND LIGHTEN IT UP
THE THINGS YOU DID TO ME, YOU´RE MAKING ME HOT
BUT I´M A MAN RELIGIOUS IN LIFE
I CUT MY BEARD AND WASH MY PRISONER´S FACE
NEXT LIFE I´LL KICK YOU OUT AND UP INTO SPACE
I WON´T FORGET THE DAY OF THE KNIFE

TAKE A PICTURE OF ME

ANOTHER DAY OF SWEET DELIGHT
I JUST HAVE WITH YOU
WE DRINK AND TALK UNTIL THE NIGHT
TELLS US WHAT TO DO

I SHOULDN´T TRY TO ACT
I´M MYSELF LIKE ROMEO
I SHOULDN´T HOLD YOU BACK
CAUSE I WANT IT GLORIOUS
TV´S STILL ON, THE RADIO IN MY HEAD

TAKE A PICTURE OF ME
FEEL MY HEARTBEAT, I NEARLY DIE
MAKE A PICTURE OF ME
AND KEEP IT TO SMILE
TAKE A PICTURE OF ME
BABY, NOW PUT THE CAM AWAY
THE SUNSHINE OF YOU
TAKES MY HEARTBEAT AWAY

I´VE HAD MY TIME, I´VE SEEN IT ALL
BODIES YOUNG AND SWEET
I MADE THEM MINE, I DID MY BEST
LIVED MY LIFE INDEED

I SHOULDN´T KEEP THE PAST IN MY MIND
NO, NOT TONIGHT
I SHOULDN´T TRY TO MOVE AWAY
NOW I SEE THE LIGHT
YOU ARE THE BEST, THE ONLY ONE THAT I SEE

TAKE A PICTURE OF ME
FEEL MY HEARTBEAT, I NEARLY DIE
MAKE A PICTURE OF ME
AND KEEP IT TO SMILE
TAKE A PICTURE OF ME
BABY, NOW PUT THE CAM AWAY
THE SUNSHINE OF YOU
TAKES MY HEARTBEAT AWAY

THE BEATING WORDS

I´M PRETTY HONEST AS I TRY TO SAY
WHAT´S GOING ON THERE IN MY MIND
DON´T WANNA HURT YOU ON ANOTHER DAY
ANOTHER TIME

I´M QUITE OUTSPOKEN WHEN IT COMES TO YOU
I NEED TO TELL YOU HOW I FEEL
IT´S REALLY HARD TO FIND SOME WORDS SO TRUE
AND THEY ARE REAL

WE SIT TOGETHER IN OUR LIVING ROOM
I TRY TO FIND THE BEATING WORDS
I MUST ADMIT IT´S NOT SO EASY NOW
BECAUSE IT HURTS
YOUR EYES THEY STARE AT ME, I´M LOSING LINES
I DON´T KNOW REALLY WHAT TO SAY
WE´VE BEEN THROUGH GOOD
AND QUITE HORRENDOUS TIMES
JUST LIKE THIS DAY

I LIKE YOU STILL BUT HEY, I LOVE YOU NOT
THE WORLD IS CHANGING SO AM I
I LOST OUR LOVE CAUSE THERE´S ANOTHER ONE
I WANNA TRY

I´M PRETTY HONEST AS I TRY TO TALK
THE TRUTH IS HARD BUT SO IS LIFE
I´M REALLY CLEAR AS NOW I TAKE THIS WALK
BACK TO ALIVE

WE SIT TOGETHER IN OUR LIVING ROOM
I TRY TO FIND THE BEATING WORDS
I MUST ADMIT IT´S NOT SO EASY NOW
BECAUSE IT HURTS
YOUR EYES THEY STARE AT ME, I´M LOSING LINES
I DON´T KNOW REALLY WHAT TO SAY
WE´VE BEEN THROUGH GOOD
AND QUITE HORRENDOUS TIMES
JUST LIKE THIS DAY

THE DEMONS IN YOU

WHOEVER PARTIES PAYS THE BILL
WHOEVER WALKS UP ON A HILL
WHOEVER DRINKS ANOTHER WINE
WHOEVER CROSSES EVERY LINE

THINKING OF YOU NOW
SINGING THIS SONG
PROBLEMS AND ANSWERS
CARRY ON

PARTIES, BIG PARTIES
I KNOW WHAT THEY DO
SMOKING WITH COCAINE
THE DEMONS IN YOU
HOLD YOU AND TOLD YOU
HOW LIFE NOW SHOULD BE
STRONGER THAN YOUR FANTASY

WHOEVER TAKES ANOTHER LINE
WHOEVER TRIES TO CHEAT ON TIME
WHOEVER LIVES INTO THE NIGHT
WHOEVER SLEEPS THE DAYS BEHIND

PAYING THE BILL NOW
FOR ALL THE WEIRD
THERE´S NO SOLUTION
I HAVE HEARD

PARTIES, BIG PARTIES
I KNOW WHAT THEY DO
SMOKING WITH COCAINE
THE DEMONS IN YOU
HOLD YOU AND TOLD YOU
HOW LIFE NOW SHOULD BE
STRONGER THAN YOUR FANTASY

THE GREEN BUTTERFLY

A BUTTERFLY COMES, HE SMILES AT ME
AND SHOWS THE WAY I HAVE TO GO
THE TREES ARE DEEP GREEN, THE FLOWERS TOO
I SEE A PRETTY RIVER FLOW

IT´S LIKE A MIRACLE
AND THOUGH I´M CRITICAL
I FOUND THIS PLACE I DON´T KNOW IF IT´S REAL
BUT HERE I FEEL ALRIGHT
I LOVE THIS GREEN OF LIGHT
I KNOW THIS PLACE IS SUCH A SPECIAL DEAL
CAN YOU FEEL THE WAY I FEEL?

AND IN THE GARDEN THERE´S A HOUSE
I HAVE THE KEY, I POP THE DOOR
I TURN INTO A LITTLE MOUSE
MY BED IS DOWN THERE ON THE FLOOR
DON´T YOU REALISE I´M THE CHOSEN ONE?
HERE I´M REALLY OUT FOR MORE

THIS BUTTERFLY FRIEND WHO CAME TO ME
I SEE HIM FLYING IN MY HOUSE
THE TREES ARE DEEP GREEN AROUND THIS PLACE
JUST PERFECT FOR THIS LITTLE MOUSE

IT´S LIKE A FANTASY
IT´S LIKE REALITY
I KNOW THE TRUTH IS SOMEWHERE IN BETWEEN
JUST LIKE THIS BUTTERFLY
JUST LIKE THIS DREAM OF MINE
I TURN AROUND AND ALL THE SCENE IS GREEN
I´M JUST LIVING IN THIS DREAM

AND IN THE GARDEN THERE´S A HOUSE
I HAVE THE KEY, I POP THE DOOR
I TURN INTO A LITTLE MOUSE
MY BED IS DOWN THERE ON THE FLOOR
DON´T YOU REALISE I´M THE CHOSEN ONE?
HERE I´M REALLY OUT FOR MORE

THE JOKER OF ALL ACES

FORGET THIS LOVE
IT'S OVER FOR ANOTHER DAY
I'VE SEEN THIS ONE
AND SHE IS NOT TOO FAR AWAY
HER EYES ARE REALLY GORGEOUS
TELL ME, ARE THEY GREEN?
I LIKE IT DARK AND DIRTY
AND A LITTLE MEAN

I START MY LITTLE JOURNEY RIGHT INTO YOUR BED
THE JOKER OF ALL ACES NO MORE BEING SAD
A NIGHT OF FUN WITHOUT YOU AND THE LONELY DAYS
FORGET THIS LOVE AND LEAVE IT AS I TURN AWAY
A NIGHT OF GOLDEN SUNSHINE MAKES A BETTER DAY
I'M FREE JUST LIKE THE OCEAN NOT SO FAR AWAY

I'M WATCHING HER
WITH HORNY WIDE UP OPEN EYES
I'M TOUCHING HER
DON'T HAVE TO ASK ABOUT HER PRICE
SHE'S WILLING AND INTERESTED
IN ANOTHER NIGHT
I SEE YOUR TEARS BUT LEAVE YOU
FOR THIS PRETTY LIGHT

I START MY LITTLE JOURNEY RIGHT INTO YOUR BED
THE JOKER OF ALL ACES NO MORE BEING SAD
A NIGHT OF FUN WITHOUT YOU AND THE LONELY DAYS
FORGET THIS LOVE AND LEAVE IT AS I TURN AWAY
A NIGHT OF GOLDEN SUNSHINE MAKES A BETTER DAY
I'M FREE JUST LIKE THE OCEAN NOT SO FAR AWAY

THE MAGIC DOOR

PAIN I FEEL
FROM INSIDE MY HEAD
I START TO CRY
MY SMILE NOW IS DEAD

CAUSE THE PAIN
IS STRONGER I FELT BEFORE
AND STILL IT GROWS MORE AND MORE
I BREAK DOWN ONTO THE FLOOR
LET ME OUT!

HOLY COW, TAKE ME NOW
SOMEWHERE I´VE BEEN BEFORE
AND AWAY FOR A DAY
WHERE I AM OUT FOR MORE
SHOW ME THE MAGIC DOOR
THROUGH TIME AND SPACE I GO
TAKE ME HOME

BACK AGAIN
THE PAIN COMES AGAIN
IT MAKES ME SCREAM
ONE HELL OF A FRIEND

IN MY MIND
I´M CALLING THE MAGIC DOOR
TO HELP ME, I´M ON THE FLOOR
THE DEVIL AND MANY MORE
TOOK CONTROL

HOLY COW, TAKE ME NOW
SOMEWHERE I´VE BEEN BEFORE
AND AWAY FOR A DAY
WHERE I AM OUT FOR MORE
SHOW ME THE MAGIC DOOR
THROUGH TIME AND SPACE I GO
TAKE ME HOME

THE WORLD IS CHANGING TO PARADISE

EVERY DAY YOU SAY THE SKY IS GREY
SO YOU DON'T SMILE AND LIVE IT ON YOUR OWN
IT'S TOO EASY, GIRL, THE WAY YOU SEE THE WORLD
DON'T UNDERSTAND YOU'RE SUCH A ROLLING STONE

I TAKE YOU SOMEWHERE DOWN THE ROAD
TO SHOW YOU PARADISE, IT'S SO NICE
I HOPE YOU OPEN UP YOUR EYES
TO SEE THE SUN AGAIN

THE WORLD IS CHANGING TO PARADISE
SEE THE TREES AND FLOWERS IN GREEN
RIGHT IN MY ARMS YOUR SICKNESS WILL FLY AWAY
JUST LIKE A DREAM
YOU START TO CARRY YOURSELF BACK HOME
TO THE PLACE I'M WAITING FOR YOU
YOU LOST YOUR SMILE
BUT BABY, YOU FOUND THE TRUTH, THE SKY IS BLUE

EVERY NIGHT YOU DIDN'T FEEL ALRIGHT
YOU CLOSED THE DOOR AND REALLY MADE ME CRY
DIDN'T GET TO YOU ALTHOUGH MY LOVE FOR YOU
WAS SO MUCH STRONGER THAN YOUR SELF-MADE LIFE

I THOUGHT YOU'RE CRAZY IN YOUR MIND
TO NOT BELIEVE IN YOU AND OUR LIFE
AND SO I'M NOW THE LUCKY ONE
THAT YOU ARE BACK ALL RIGHT

THE WORLD IS CHANGING TO PARADISE
SEE THE TREES AND FLOWERS IN GREEN
RIGHT IN MY ARMS YOUR SICKNESS WILL FLY AWAY
JUST LIKE A DREAM
YOU START TO CARRY YOURSELF BACK HOME
TO THE PLACE I'M WAITING FOR YOU
YOU LOST YOUR SMILE
BUT BABY, YOU FOUND THE TRUTH, THE SKY IS BLUE

THERE'S A BOY

YOU'RE LOOKING WEIRD, YOU'RE FEELING STRANGE
YOUR LIFE WILL CHANGE INTO ANOTHER ONE
YOU'RE GAINING WEIGHT, YOU ALWAYS SLEEP
YOU'RE LOOKING PALE
AND WEAK YOU'RE ON YOUR FEET

HEADACHE'S STRONG, YOUR BELLY STARTS TO HURT
I'VE NEVER SEEN RED TEARS UP IN YOUR FACE
CALLING DR. NO TO HELP YOU OUT TO HEAR THE TRUTH

THERE'S A BOY RIGHT INSIDE YOUR BELLY SWEET
THERE A BOY, AS YOU'RE PREGNANT TAKE A SEAT
OH HAPPY DAY!
DR. NO, HELP US TO REGAIN CONTROL
IT'S A BOY SO SWEET, I LOVE YOU ALL
INTO ANOTHER LIFE WE JUST DRIFT AWAY
WELL, THERE'S A BOY

I'VE NEVER SEEN YOU ON THE FLOOR
CALLING FOR HELP, YOU COULDN'T TAKE NO MORE
YOU'VE CHANGED A LOT, I DIDN'T KNOW
ABOUT A BOY WHO'S WAITING FOR THE SHOW

DOCTOR CAME AND CHECKED YOU IN THE NIGHT
HE TURNED AROUND, SMILED RIGHT INTO MY EYES
PUT HIS DOCTOR BAG AWAY AND SAID: I WILL BE DAD

THERE'S A BOY RIGHT INSIDE YOUR BELLY SWEET
THERE A BOY, AS YOU'RE PREGNANT TAKE A SEAT
OH HAPPY DAY!
DR. NO, HELP US TO REGAIN CONTROL
IT'S A BOY SO SWEET, I LOVE YOU ALL
INTO ANOTHER LIFE WE JUST DRIFT AWAY
WELL, THERE'S A BOY

HEY, I LOVE YOUR EYES
I LOVE YOUR SMILE, I LOVE YOUR FACE
YOU WILL BE MY ONE
SO MANY WAYS

TIME COMES AGAIN

TIME COMES AGAIN
FINE WHO I AM
LIFE IS TOO HARD
I WILL BE, I WILL BE
SOME DIFFERENT MAN
IN MY LIFE FUTURE TREE

TIMES COMES AGAIN
I CAN MAKE IT SO MUCH BETTER
TRYING AGAIN
WALKING AROUND THROUGH THE DOOR
LIFE GIVES ME CHANCE
TO UNDO AND TO FORGIVE SOME
NOW HERE I AM
FOR A NEW START OF MY LIFE
AND AWAY

HOPE IN MY HEART
STRONG FOR A START
NOW ONE MORE TIME
ONE MORE TRY ON THE LINE
GOD, HERE I AM
JUST FOR YOU ONCE AGAIN

TIMES COMES AGAIN
I CAN MAKE IT SO MUCH BETTER
TRYING AGAIN
WALKING AROUND THROUGH THE DOOR
LIFE GIVES ME CHANCE
TO UNDO AND TO FORGIVE SOME
NOW HERE I AM
FOR A NEW START OF MY LIFE
AND AWAY

DREAMS, NO MORE DREAMS
ON MY WAY, ON MY WAY
SCENES OF A MAN
ON HIS WAY NOW TO STAY

TRÄUME IM MÄRCHENKLEID

ICH SITZ AM MEER UND TAUCH HINEIN
IN EINE ANDERE WELT
EIN HELLER STRAHL TRIFFT MICH GANZ SANFT
UND ZEIGT MIR WAS MIR GEFÄLLT

DAS WASSER WIRD ZU EINEM WALD
MIT BÄUMEN SO GROSS WIE WIR
ICH SEH DICH SCHON, MEIN PRINZ, JETZT BIN ICH BEI DIR
JETZT BIN ICH ENDLICH HIER!

TRÄUME KÖNNEN GESCHEHEN
TRÄUME KÖNNEN VERGEHEN
DARUM SEI STETS BEREIT
TRÄUME IM MÄRCHENKLEID

IN DIESER WELT WO ZÄRTLICHKEIT
UND LIEBE SICH BERÜHREN
WO HEITERKEIT IST STETS BEREIT
WO MANN UND FRAU SICH VERFÜHREN

HIER LEBE ICH IN MEINEM WALD
EIN LEBEN IM PARADIES
BIS PLÖTZLICH MICH DER HELLE STRAHL WIEDER TRIFFT
UND FORT MEINE LIEBE IST

TRÄUME KÖNNEN GESCHEHEN
TRÄUME KÖNNEN VERGEHEN
DARUM SEI STETS BEREIT
LASS ES EINFACH GESCHEHEN
DU MUSST ES GAR NICHT VERSTEHEN
TROTZDEM SEI STETS BEREIT
TRÄUME IM MÄRCHENKLEID

EIN NEUER TAG, EIN NEUES GLÜCK
ICH WARTE IM MÄRCHENKLEID
DAS WASSER IST NOCH STILL DOCH ICH BIN BEREIT
SCHLEUS MICH DURCH RAUM UND ZEIT

UND ALLES WAS GESCHIEHT
(DAS DARF GESCHEHEN)

DAS RENDEZVOUS IM KERZENSCHEIN
UND KÖSTLICH IST DER WEIN
HAND IN HAND AM MÄRCHENSTRAND
IM GOLD-GELBEN SAND
DER ABENDGANG ROMANTIK PUR
ICH SCHENK DIR MEINE HAND
DIE DU ZÄRTLICH WARM UMSCHLIESST
WIE DÜNEN DEN SAND

UND ALLES WAS GESCHIEHT
DAS DARF GESCHEHEN DENN ES BERÜHRT
MEIN KLEINES HERZ SPRINGT HOCH EMPOR
UND STRAHLT DICH AN
DIE LIEBE DIE ICH SPÜR
UND WÄHREND ICH DICH JETZT BERÜHR
WIRD MIR SO KLAR DASS ICH DIR GEHÖR
FÜR IMMER MEHR

DIE ZÄRTLICHKEIT, DIE DU MIR SCHENKST
SCHENKT MIR DAS PARADIES
DEINE NÄHE GIBT MIR HALT
DEIN KUSS SCHMECKT SO SÜSS
MEIN DEPRI-TIEF IST LÄNGST VORBEI
VERGESSEN ALLERLEI
NUR NOCH DU, DU ZÄHLST FÜR MICH
OH, ICH LIEBE DICH

UND ALLES WAS GESCHIEHT
DAS DARF GESCHEHEN DENN ES BERÜHRT
MEIN KLEINES HERZ SPRINGT HOCH EMPOR
UND STRAHLT DICH AN
DIE LIEBE DIE ICH SPÜR
UND WÄHREND ICH DICH JETZT BERÜHR
WIRD MIR SO KLAR DASS ICH DIR GEHÖR
FÜR IMMER MEHR

WIE EINE ROSE DIE ERWACHT
SO STRAHLE ICH DICH AN HEUT NACHT

UNENDLICHKEIT

DIE ERDE IST RUND, WIR DREHEN UNS MIT IHR
SEIT GERAUMER ZEIT
WIR WERDEN GEBOREN UND ZU ASCHE IM STAUB
UNENDLICHKEIT
WIR LEBEN ZU SCHNELL UND WIR STERBEN ZU JUNG
ALLES WAS UNS BLEIBT
ERINNERUNGEN UND GEFÜHLE AN DIE ZEIT

UND ICH SCHAUE AUF DIE UHR
KURZ VOR 12
WIEDER IST EIN TAG HERUM
ALL DAS GELD
ALL DER LUXUS, ALL DIE MACHT
HELFEN NICHT
DIE UNENDLICHKEIT
DIE KENNT AUCH DEIN GESICHT

ICH WAR MAL EIN KIND, ICH BIN NUN EIN MANN
MENSCH, DIE ZEIT VERGEHT
ICH FÜHLE MICH JUNG DOCH MEIN KÖRPER DER SAGT:
ALLES TUT WEH!
DIE SANDUHR SIE LÄUFT, MEIN WEG IST NOCH LANG
ALLES SCHON GESEHEN
UND TROTZDEM GENIESS ICH, MEIN LEBEN IST SO SCHÖN

UND ICH SCHAU WIEDER AUF DIE UHR
MITTERNACHT
UND WIEDER IST EIN TAG HERUM
DIESE NACHT
IST WIRKLICH EINZIGARTIG SCHÖN
DENN ICH WEISS
DIE UNENDLICHKEIT
DIE KOMMT UM JEDEN PREIS

UP IN THE PLACE OF LOVE

WHEN I SLEEP RIGHT IN YOUR ARMS
THE WORLD STANDS STILL BUT NOT MY HEART
SINCE THAT DAY YOU SHOWED ME HOME
I´M NOT ALONE

IN MY DREAMS I FLY WITH YOU
TO SEE THE WORLD, THE GREEN AND BLUE
IN BETWENN WE KISS AND LOVE
RIGHT ON THE STARS

UP IN THE PLACE OF LOVE
HERE IN THE SKY ABOVE
LONELY WE ARE FOR SURE
BUT NOT ALONE
SHOW ME YOUR MAGIC EYES AND TAKE ME
TOUCH ME AGAIN, SWEET GIRL, AND MAKE ME
HAPPY WITH YOU
FOREVER ON THE STARS

LONG BEFORE, I WAS A CLOWN
A FOOL OF LOVE, GOT PUSHED AROUND
NEVER THOUGHT I´D FIND A GIRL
A ONE LIKE YOU

PEARLY GATES I´VE SEEN BEFORE
BUT THIS ONE TIME AN OPEN DOOR
LET ME IN INTO YOUR HEART
THE STORY GOES

UP IN THE PLACE OF LOVE
HERE IN THE SKY ABOVE
LONELY WE ARE FOR SURE
BUT NOT ALONE
SHOW ME YOUR MAGIC EYES AND TAKE ME
TOUCH ME AGAIN, SWEET GIRL, AND MAKE ME
HAPPY WITH YOU
FOREVER ON THE STARS

V - Z

VISIONS OF LOVE
(ARE HERE AGAIN)

VISIONS OF LOVE ARE HERE AGAIN
OR SO IT SEEMS
LOVERS APART UNITE AGAIN
REALITY DREAMS

LEAVING THE PROBLEMS
IN OUR WORLD BEHIND
TRYING TO MAKE IT BETTER
ONE MORE TIME

COME BACK INTO MY LIFE
I´M FEELING SO STRONG FOR YOU
I´M MISSING YOUR TOUCH, I DO
TRY NOT TO FALL AGAIN
I MADE UP MY MIND TO BE TRUE
WILL GIVE ALL MY LOVE JUST FOR YOU
VISIONS OF LOVE
VISIONS OF LOVE

VISIONS OF LOVE ARE STRONG AGAIN
THEY MAKE ME FLY
AS I JUST HOLD YOUR HAND AGAIN
THE WORLD WILL GO BY

LEAVING THE THOUGHTS
OF WOE AND HATE BEHIND
AND NOW AHEAD OF US
ARE BETTER TIMES

COME BACK INTO MY LIFE
I´M FEELING SO STRONG FOR YOU
I´M MISSING YOUR TOUCH, I DO
TRY NOT TO FALL AGAIN
I MADE UP MY MIND TO BE TRUE
WILL GIVE ALL MY LOVE JUST FOR YOU
VISIONS OF LOVE
VISIONS OF LOVE

WARLORD OF THE BRAVE

THE FIRST ONE WAS THE PERFECT YEAR FOR ME
YOU GAVE ME ALL YOU HAD AND EVEN MORE
MADE ME SO HAPPY IN YOUR ARMS, COULD IT BE?

THE SECOND YEAR WAS STRONG ENOUGH TO STAY
ALTHOUGH YOU CHANGED INTO ANOTHER ONE
YOU MADE ME CRY AND LIVED YOUR LIFE, WHAT A FOOL!

YOUR DESIRE GETTING LOST
YOU LEFT ME EVERY NIGHT
TIME WILL BRING BACK ALL I WANT
THE SUNNY TIMES AHEAD

THE WARLORD OF THE BRAVE IS CHANGING THE SCENE
THE THIRD YEAR AND THE FORTH WERE UGLY AND MEAN
SHE CHANGED INTO A DRAGON KILLING MY DREAM
THE PROBLEM THAT I HAVE IS SIMPLE BUT CRUEL
I LOST MY BUCKS TO HER, SHE MADE ME A FOOL
I LOST MY LIFE TO HER BUT NOW IT´S TOO LATE

YOUR HANDS WERE SOFT AND FRESH WAS OUR LOVE
YOU KISSED ME 700 TIMES A DAY
I FELL FOR YOU AND DIDN´T GO, FLYIN´ HIGH

THE THINGS WE DID IN BED MADE ME BELIEVE
YOUR LOVE MUST BE THE BIGGEST OF ´EM ALL
BUT SOON I SAW THE OTHER FACE CREEPIN´ OUT

DARK THE CLOUDS ARE IN THE SKY
THE THUNDER AND THE RAIN
WELL, MY SOUL IS GETTING LOST
I REALLY WONDER WHY

THE WARLORD OF THE BRAVE IS CHANGING THE SCENE
THE THIRD YEAR AND THE FORTH WERE UGLY AND MEAN
SHE CHANGED INTO A DRAGON KILLING MY DREAM
THE PROBLEM THAT I HAVE IS SIMPLE BUT CRUEL
I LOST MY BUCKS TO HER, SHE MADE ME A FOOL
I LOST MY LIFE TO HER BUT NOW IT´S TOO LATE

WAS HAB ICH GETAN?

ATEMLOS NACH DIESER NACHT
ICH RUF DICH AN
WAR ES FÜR DICH AUCH SO SCHÖN?
GEH ENDLICH RAN

DOCH ICH WARTE UMSONST
DENN DER ABC
SPULT DIE LEIER VON VORN
DAS TUT WEH

WAS HAB ICH GETAN? SAG MIR WARUM
GEHST DU NICHT RAN, DAS BRINGT MICH UM!
WAR ES NICHT SCHÖN IN MEINEM ARM?
IN MEINEM BETT? TU MIR DAS NICHT AN!
ICH LIEBE DICH

HOFFNUNGSVOLL, EIN NEUER TAG
ICH RUF DICH AN
WILLST DU MIT MIR GLÜCKLICH SEIN?
GEH ENDLICH RAN

WIEDER DIESER MOMENT
DER MICH EWIG QUÄLT
DIESER EINE MOMENT
DER FÜR MICH ZÄHLT

WAS HAB ICH GETAN? SAG MIR WARUM
GEHST DU NICHT RAN, DAS BRINGT MICH UM!
WAR ES NICHT SCHÖN IN MEINEM ARM?
IN MEINEM BETT? TU MIR DAS NICHT AN!
ICH LIEBE DICH

NICHT EINMAL EIN WORT
NACH DIESER WUNDERSCHÖNEN NACHT
SITZ ICH AN DER BAR
UND RUF DICH WIEDER AN HEUT NACHT

WELCOME ME HOME

FAR AWAY I WAS, NOW BACK AGAIN JUST FOR YOU
I MISSED YOU EVERY DAY I WAS IN THE BLUE
EVERY DAY I SAID „I LOVE YOU, GIRL" ON THE PHONE
HAD TO SLEEP WITHOUT YOUR BODY CLOSE ON MY OWN
WELL, TOMORROW I´LL BE BACK AGAIN JUST FOR YOU
I´M SURE I´LL NEVER EVER BE WITHOUT YOU
A HOMECOMIN´ MAN
MISSING YOUR TOUCH AND YOUR KISS
YOU AND YOUR BODY I MISS

ON MY WAY TO YOU I OPEN UP THE FRONT DOOR
AND THERE YOU ARE AND SMILE AT ME, I WANT MORE
BUT THE FIRST THING I CAN SEE IN HER PRETTY HANDS
IS HER SMARTPHONE AND SHE´S TELLING ME IT´S HER FRIENDS
COULD IT BE SHE´S REALLY CRAZY UP IN HER MIND?
I THOUGHT SHE LEFT THE NEED OF THIS FAR BEHIND
I´M ANGRY FOR TWO
DON´T WANNA CUDDLE WITH YOU
FEELING SO SAD AND SO BLUE

ALTHOUGH I´M CRAZY FOR YOU, BETTER LEAVE ME ALONE
THOUGHT YOU´D BE ONLY AND LONELY TO WELCOME ME HOME
SHIT ON THE OTHERS, YOU HAD SO MUCH TIME FOR THE PHONE
DON´T THINK IT´S LOVE
WHEN YOU STUPIDLY WELCOME ME HOME

AS I SMASH THE DOOR I TAKE A SEAT IN MY ROOM
I THOUGHT SHE´D BE A BETTER ONE VERY SOON
BUT AS LONG AS I AM WAITING NOW SHE DON´T COME
GUESS SHE´S STILL A LITTLE PRISONER HAVING FUN
AS I NEED TO KNOW I SEE HER HANDS ON THE PHONE
SHE SMILES AND LIVES HER LIFE AGAIN ON HER OWN
NO FEELINGS FOR ME
BETTER I LEAVE HER ALONE
SOMEWHERE I REALLY DON´T KNOW

ALTHOUGH I´M CRAZY FOR YOU BETTER LEAVE ME ALONE
THOUGHT YOU´D BE ONLY AND LONELY TO WELCOME ME HOME
SHIT ON THE OTHERS, YOU HAD SO MUCH TIME FOR THE PHONE
DON´T THINK IT´S LOVE
WHEN YOU STUPIDLY WELCOME ME HOME

WER DU BIST

IST DIE WELT DIESELBE OHNE MICH?
IST DIE NACHT DIESELBE OHNE DICH?

EINE NACHT KANN ALLES ÄNDERN
WIE DER TAG
IRGENDWANN
WENN ICH ZU DIR SAG:

16 JAHRE UND MEHR
WILLKOMMEN IM PARADIES
IST ES WIRKLICH SO SCHÖN?
ICH WEISS GENAU WER DU BIST
JA, DIE REISE ZU ZWEIT
DIE ENDET AN JENEM TAG
WENN DER PROPHET MICH ERLEUCHTET
BLEIB ICH STARK

IST DIE LIEBE EHRLICH ODER NICHT?
KÜSST DU WIRKLICH ZÄRTLICH MEIN GESICHT?

DIESE HUNDERTTAUSEND FRAGEN
STELL ICH MIR
JEDE NACHT
JEDEN TAG EIN BIER

16 JAHRE UND MEHR
WILLKOMMEN IM PARADIES
IST ES WIRKLICH SO SCHÖN?
ICH WEISS GENAU WER DU BIST
JA, DIE REISE ZU ZWEIT
DIE ENDET AN JENEM TAG
WENN DER PROPHET MICH ERLEUCHTET
BLEIB ICH STARK

WER KANN SAGEN WAS MORGEN KOMMT?

ICH BIN TRAURIG, ES ZIEHT MICH RAUS
NACH DER TRENNUNG ALLEIN ZU HAUS
DOCH ICH SCHAU NACH VORN

ALL DIE TRAUER DIE ICH VERSPÜR
ALL DIE TRÄNEN DIE MICH BERÜHREN
VORBEI, ICH BIN FREI

WER KANN SAGEN WAS MORGEN KOMMT?
EINE GARANTIE FÜR DIE GROSSE LIEBE GIBT ES NIE
UM DIE ECKE DA WARTET SIE
DU MUSST SIE NUR SEHEN
SEI BEREIT FÜR MORGEN
UND DIE WELT WIRD WIEDER SCHÖN

WENN DER SCHATTEN VORÜBERZIEHT
UND EIN HERZ SICH IN MICH VERLIEBT
JA, DANN BIN ICH FREI

NEUE LIEBE, EIN NEUES GLÜCK
ICH SCHAU VORWÄRTS, DENK NICHT ZURÜCK
MEIN HERZ LEBT DEN TRAUM

WER KANN SAGEN WAS MORGEN KOMMT?
EINE GARANTIE FÜR DIE GROSSE LIEBE GIBT ES NIE
UM DIE ECKE DA WARTET SIE
DU MUSST SIE NUR SEHEN
SEI BEREIT FÜR MORGEN
UND DIE WELT WIRD WIEDER SCHÖN

WESTERLAND

EBBE UND FLUT SIND WIE TAUBEN IM WIND
KOMMEN UM DANN ZU GEHEN
NICHTS IST SO SCHÖN
WIE AM SAMSTAG IM WIND ZU STEHEN

EBBE UND FLUT, DIE GEZEITEN ZU SEHEN
ICH FÜHL MICH GUT ERHOLT
NICHTS IST SO SCHÖN
WIE EIN ABEND AM STRAND ZU STEHEN

ZWISCHEN EBBE UND FLUT HIER AM STRAND
ZWISCHEN DÜNEN UND GRÜN - WESTERLAND
HIER TANK ICH KRAFT, TANKE AUF
ZWISCHEN EBBE UND FLUT, ICH FAHR HINAUS
HINAUS AUF DIE SEE WEG VOM STRAND
DIE CHAMPS-ÉLYSÉES - WESTERLAND
ICH TANKE KRAFT KOMMT DIE FLUT
OH WESTERLAND, DU TUST MIR GUT

EBBE UND FLUT SIND WIE SONNE UND MOND
SPIELEN EIN SPIEL MIT MIR
NICHTS IST SO SCHÖN
WIE EIN ABENTEUER MIT DIR

EBBE UND FLUT SIND WIE FRÜHLING UND HERBST
SOMMER- UND WINTERZEIT
NICHTS IST SO SCHÖN
WIE EIN ABEND AM STRAND ZU ZWEIT

ZWISCHEN EBBE UND FLUT HIER AM STRAND
ZWISCHEN DÜNEN UND GRÜN - WESTERLAND
HIER TANK ICH KRAFT, TANKE AUF
ZWISCHEN EBBE UND FLUT, ICH FAHR HINAUS
HINAUS AUF DIE SEE WEG VOM STRAND
DIE CHAMPS-ÉLYSÉES - WESTERLAND
ICH TANKE KRAFT KOMMT DIE FLUT
OH WESTERLAND, DU TUST MIR GUT

WHATEVER IT MAY TAKE

WHATEVER IT MAY TAKE TO BE THE HERO OF THE WORLD
I TRY TO FIND SOMETHING LIKE THE KEY
WHATEVER IT MAY TAKE FOR ME TO FIND A PRETTY GIRL
I SEARCH THE LIGHT I JUST WANNA SEE

CHANCES, NEVER HAD MY CHANCES
NEVER HAD SOME FRIENDS AS LIFE TOOK ME AWAY
FLYING TO A DIFFERENT ISLE AND
HERE I'M ALWAYS SMILING UP FROM THIS DAY

LIKE THE PICTURE IN MY HEART
LIKE THE TIGER AND THE BUTTERFLIES
LIKE THE PICTURE IN MY MIND
HERE I GO, OH BABY, RUN THE SHOW
LIKE A PICTURE FULL OF LOVE
LIKE A TIGER EATING BUTTERFLIES
LIKE A CATFISH IN DISGUISE
RUN AWAY INTO ANOTHER DAY

WHATEVER IT MAY TAKE TO FIND A LITTLE BIT OF LUCK
I GIVE IT ALL, GIVE MY VERY BEST
WHATEVER IT MAY TAKE FOR ME I'M NEVER GIVING UP
I LIVE IT ALL BETTER THAN THE REST

DARKNESS, RIGHT INTO THE DARKNESS
I JUST KNOW MY HEART IS LOSING MORE AND MORE
CRYING, AM I REALLY CRYING?
MAYBE I AM DYING UP ON THE FLOOR

LIKE THE PICTURE IN MY HEART
LIKE THE TIGER AND THE BUTTERFLIES
LIKE THE PICTURE IN MY MIND
HERE I GO, OH BABY, RUN THE SHOW
LIKE A PICTURE FULL OF LOVE
LIKE A TIGER EATING BUTTERFLIES
LIKE A CATFISH IN DISGUISE
RUN AWAY INTO ANOTHER DAY

WILL YOU LIVE YOUR LIFE WITH ME?

ON THE STAGE I AM TONIGHT
AND THE LIGHTS ARE SHINING BRIGHT FOR YOU
PURPLE LOVE IS IN THE AIR
AND PRETTY FACES EVERYWHERE, IT´S TRUE

I CRASHED THIS PARTY IN THE NIGHT
YOU DIDN´T KNOW MY PLAN
TO TIGHTEN OUR LOVE
AND SO I ASK YOU
UNDERNEATH THE STARS ABOVE:

WILL YOU LIVE YOUR LIFE WITH ME
UNTIL THE END OF OUR DAYS?
WHEN WE LEAVE THIS WORLD TO PURPLE HAZE
WILL YOU LOVE ME DAYS AND NIGHTS
THROUGH THE WRONGS AND THROUGH THE RIGHTS?
AS I TAKE YOUR HAND AND KISS YOUR FACE
MARRY ME, MY GIRL, AMAZING GRAZE

ALL THE FACES I CAN SEE
THEY BELIEVE IN YOU AND ME TONIGHT
I JUST CRASHED THIS PARTY SCENE
AND TRY TO REALISE MY DREAM THIS NIGHT

I KNOW I´M CRAZY JUST FOR YOU
AND ALL THE THINGS I WANNA DO
WITH YOU AGAIN
AND SO I ASK YOU:
WILL YOU TAKE ME AS YOUR MAN?

WILL YOU LIVE YOUR LIFE WITH ME
UNTIL THE END OF OUR DAYS?
WHEN WE LEAVE THIS WORLD TO PURPLE HAZE
WILL YOU LOVE ME DAYS AND NIGHTS
THROUGH THE WRONGS AND THROUGH THE RIGHTS?
AS I TAKE YOUR HAND AND KISS YOUR FACE
MARRY ME, MY GIRL, AMAZING GRAZE

WHERE IS THE SUN?

THE SUN IS ABOUT TO COVER THE SKY
BUT SOMETHING IS STRANGE TONIGHT
SOME TICKLES OF SNOW ARE FALLING AGAIN
WITH TEARDROPS OF RAIN SO HIGH
NO MORE SUN

RAINY
WHERE IS THE SUN?
NOW THAT THE MORNING HAS JUST BEGUN
SCARY
MOMENTS WITH YOU
THE SKY IS JUST BLACK, NOT BLUE

I CLOSE ALL THE DOORS
I SWITCH ON THE LIGHTS
MY BED IS THE PLACE TO BE
THE END OF THE DAYS
THE WORLD AND THE WAYS
IS SOMETHING I CANNOT SEE
BUT I FEEL

RAINY
WHERE IS THE SUN?
NOW THAT THE MORNING HAS JUST BEGUN
SCARY
MOMENTS WITH YOU
THE SKY IS JUST BLACK, NOT BLUE

HOLD ME
HOLD ME ONE MORE TIME
DARKNESS NOW IS HERE TO SHINE
MAYBE
ON A SUNNY DAY
THINGS AGAIN WILL BE OK

WOHER DIESER BLICK?
(OHNE LIEBE)

SAG MIR WOHER DIESER BLICK KOMMT
UND WARUM?
SAG MIR WIESO DU JETZT SCHWEIGST
TRAURIG UND STUMM
WAR ES DER ABEND
ALS ICH WOANDERS SCHLIEF?
WAR ES DER MORGEN
ALS MICH EIN ANDERER RIEF?

WOHER DIESER BLICK OHNE LIEBE?
WAS HAB ICH DIR DENN GETAN?
SAG MIR EINFACH WANN UND WIESO
DOCH SCHWEIG MICH NICHT AN!
WOHER DIESER BLICK OHNE LIEBE?
ICH WEISS WIRKLICH KEINEN GRUND
BITTE HILF MIR AUF MEINE BEINE
MEIN HERZ IST SO WUND

WIR SITZEN UNS GEGENÜBER
UND SCHWEIGEN UNS AN
TRAURIG UND STUMM DIESER BLICK
DU MACHST MICH KRANK!
SCHREI MICH DOCH AN
ODER MACH GANZ EINFACH SCHLUSS
ALLES NOCH BESSER
BEVOR ICH WEINEN MUSS

WOHER DIESER BLICK OHNE LIEBE?
WAS HAB ICH DIR DENN GETAN?
SAG MIR EINFACH WANN UND WIESO
DOCH SCHWEIG MICH NICHT AN!
WOHER DIESER BLICK OHNE LIEBE?
ICH WEISS WIRKLICH KEINEN GRUND
BITTE HILF MIR AUF MEINE BEINE
MEIN HERZ IST SO WUND

WOLF

OH SWEET MARIE
I COME AND GO
I PLAY MY GAME
I RUN THE SHOW
THAT´S HOW IT GOES

OH SWEET JUSTINE
I´M HERE FOR YOU
I KNOW FOR SURE
YOU LOVE ME TOO
I´M HERE AGAIN

I´M JUST A MAN
LIKE A WOLF HERE I AM
GIVE ME YOUR LOVE
MAKE IT FEEL GOOD ENOUGH
THEN I WILL COME BACK

CASSANDRA CUTE
YOU ARE THE ONE
I´D LIKE TO BE
FROM NOW TIL 1
WITH YOU AGAIN

OH JADE AND JILL
THE HIGHLIGHT SIS´
IT´S TWO FOR ONE
A DOUBLE KISS
A SPECIAL NIGHT

I´M JUST A MAN
LIKE A WOLF HERE I AM
GIVE ME YOUR LOVE
MAKE IT FEEL GOOD ENOUGH
THEN I WILL BE BACK

WORLD IS MINE

LATE AT NIGHT
WHAT A DREAM I HAD TO DREAM!
COMES THE LIGHT
NIGHTMARE´S OVER AND IT SEEMS

BORN I´M AGAIN IN A TIME
PEOPLE HAVE GONE
WORLD IS MINE

I´M KING OF THE WORLD
PLAYING ALONG WITH YOU
CREATING A GIRL
BEAUTIFUL AND SO TRUE
LIVE IN THIS WORLD WITH YOU
TIL DARKNESS FALLS

WORLD IS MINE
HAPPY I ENJOY MY TIME
RULE THIS WORLD
BY MY SIDE A PRETTY GIRL

KISSES OF GOLD IN MY MOUTH
BUILDING THIS WHITE
PALACE HOUSE

I´M KING OF THE WORLD
PLAYING ALONG WITH YOU
I´M HERE WITH THIS GIRL
BEAUTIFUL AND SO TRUE
LIVE IN THIS WORLD WITH YOU
TIL DARKNESS FALLS

HUNDREDS OF LIVES GOING BY
NOW THIS ONE LIFE
TAKES ME HIGH

YOU ARE MY ETERNITY

AS THE SUN GOES DOWN I SEE YOU SHINE
LIKE A CRYTAL BALL UP IN THE SKY
AS THE MOONLIGHT FLICKERS IN YOUR EYES
UNTIL THE MORNING COMES YOU´RE SO ALIVE

IF SOMEONE TRIES TO BREAKING US APART
IF SOMEONE HOPES WE´RE LOSING OUR LOVE
HE´S WRONG TO SAY

AS THE LIGHT TURNS BLUE I SEE YOU FLY
LIKE A SUPERGIRL UP IN THE SKY
AS THE MAGIC LIFTS ME UP TO YOU
LIKE A SUPERMAN UP IN THE BLUE

IF SOMEONE´S THERE TO VANISH OUR DREAM
IF SOMEONE TRIES TO CHANGE THIS PRETTY SCENE
HE´S WRONG TO TRY

YOU ARE MY ETERNITY
MY ONLY LOVE AND NOT JUST A FANTASY
I SWEAR BY ALL THE STARS ABOVE
IT´S YOU I LOVE

AS THE DAYLIGHT THROWS YOU FAR AWAY
I GET DOWN TO EARTH AND LIVE MY DAY
BUT I KNOW FOR SURE THE NIGHT WILL COME
AND AS THE SUN GOES DOWN I KNOW IT´S DONE

WE REUNITE AND HAVE ANOTHER NIGHT
I KISS AND HOLD YOU TIL THE MORNING LIGHT
ENDS OUR DREAM

YOU ARE MY ETERNITY
MY ONLY LOVE AND NOT JUST A FANTASY
I SWEAR BY ALL THE STARS ABOVE
IT´S YOU I LOVE

YOU ARE THE ONE FOR ME

I´VE SEEN IT JUST ALL
A RISE AND A FALL
BUT THIS ONE IS NEW FOR ME
A LOVE THAT´S SO STRONG
I KEEP HOLDING ON
A VISION, A FANTASY
I CANNOT BELIEVE
THIS FEELINGS ARE REAL
THEN I DREAM AWAY
YOU´RE HOLDING ME CLOSE
BABY, I´VE GOT TO SAY:

YOU ARE THE ONE FOR ME
ALL YOUR LOVE AND YOUR HEART I SEE
WE ARE SO CLOSE EVERY DAY EVEN MORE
I AM THE ONE FOR YOU
AND I KNOW THAT YOU LOVE ME TOO
ALL OF MY DREAMS WILL BE REAL LIVING FOR

A SCHOOL AFTER 8
WAS WORKING SO LATE
I FINISHED AND TURNED AROUND
WAS STARING AT YOU
YOUR EYES CAUGHT UP TOO
I FELT LIKE A KING GETS CROWNED
WAS TAKING YOU OUT
A RISE AND A SHOUT
WE WERE OH SO SURE
WE CARRIED THIS ON
NOW WE ARE OUT FOR MORE

YOU ARE THE ONE FOR ME
ALL YOUR LOVIN´ YOU GIVE TO ME
WE ARE SO CLOSE EVERY NIGHT, EVERY DAY
I AM THE ONE FOR YOU
AND I KNOW HOW YOU LOVE ME TOO
HERE BY YOUR SIDE NOW WITH YOU I WILL STAY

ZU DIR ZURÜCK

DIE LEEREN WORTE DIE DU SAGST
TUN MIR WEH, TUN MIR WEH
UND DIESER SCHMERZ IN MEINER BRUST
LÄSST MICH GEHEN, LÄSST MICH GEHEN

DOCH DEINE AUGEN NIEMALS LÜGEN
UND DU WEISST ICH LIEBE DICH
HALT MICH ZURÜCK UND BEWEIS MIR
DASS DU MICH WIRKLICH VERMISST

UND DANN KOMM ICH ZU DIR ZURÜCK
ZU DIR ZURÜCK
HALTE MICH FEST
SONST WERD ICH HEUT NACHT VERRÜCKT
ICH WERD VERRÜCKT
EIN NEUES LEBEN FÜR UNS ZWEI
EIN NEUES LEBEN FÜR UNS ZWEI
DENN NUR MIT DIR KANN ICH WIRKLICH GLÜCKLICH SEIN
GLÜCKLICH SEIN

DIE SCHÖNEN WORTE DIE DU SAGST JETZT ZU MIR
DIE SCHÖNEN WORTE
ICH DRÜCKE DICH GANZ FEST AN MICH
UND ICH SPÜR, JA, ICH SPÜR

DU BIST MEIN SCHICKSAL, MEINE LIEBE
NUR ZUSAMMEN SIND WIR EINS
KÜSS MICH GANZ ZART UND BEWEIS MIR
DASS DU ES WIRKLICH EHRLICH MEINST

UND DANN KOMM ICH ZU DIR ZURÜCK
ZU DIR ZURÜCK
HALTE MICH FEST
SONST WERD ICH HEUT NACHT VERRÜCKT
ICH WERD VERRÜCKT
EIN NEUES LEBEN FÜR UNS ZWEI
EIN NEUES LEBEN FÜR UNS ZWEI
DENN NUR MIT DIR KANN ICH WIRKLICH GLÜCKLICH SEIN
GLÜCKLICH SEIN